MOSES

GOD'S FAITHFUL SERVANT

BOOKS BY CYRIL J. BARBER

Successful Church Libraries, with E. Towns
The Minister's Library, 2 vols.
The Minister's Library, vol. 3, with M. L. Bickley
God Has the Answer
Searching for Identity
Nehemiah: An Expositional Commentary
Always a Winner, with J. Carter
Vital Encounter
Marriage Enrichment in the Church
Leadership: The Dynamics of Success, with G. Strauss
Introduction to Theological.Research
Your Marriage Has Real Possibilities
Ruth: A Story of God's Grace
You Can Have a Happy Marriage
Habakkuk and Zephaniah
Through the Valley of Tears
Your Marriage Can Last a Lifetime
Judges: A Narrative of God's Power
The Books of Samuel, 2 vols.
Best Books for your Home ... Library
Introduction to Theological Research, rev. ed., with R. Krauss, Jr.
Unlocking the Scriptures
Faithfulness of God, 2 vols.
The Books of Kings, 4 vols. in 2.
The Dynamics of Effective Leadership
The Books of Chronicles, 2 vols.
Lord, Please Help Me, My Teenager Is Driving Me Crazy, with G. Strauss
Joshua: We Will Serve the Lord
Ezra and Esther
Profiles of the Patriarchs, 3 vols. (Abraham & Isaac; Jacob; Joseph)
My Son, Jonah, with G. Strauss
Moses: God's Faithful Servant
Contributor, *Zondervan Pictorial Encyclopedia of the Bible*
Contributor, *New Unger's Bible Dictionary*
Contributor, *Baker's Encyclopedia of the Bible*

MOSES

GOD'S FAITHFUL SERVANT

A Brief Profile

by

CYRIL J. BARBER

WIPF & STOCK · Eugene, Oregon

Wipf and Stock Publishers
199 W 8th Ave, Suite 3
Eugene, OR 97401

Moses: God's Faithful Servant
A Brief Profile
By Barber, Cyril J.
Copyright©2012 by Barber, Cyril J.
ISBN 13: 978-1-49826-322-1
Publication date 3/1/2012

CONTENTS

PREFACE

PREFACE

A recent observer of current literary mores stated that contemporary writers are like pygmies who stand on the shoulders of giants of the past. I agree. While in seminary I had the opportunity to study under some of the godliest men who ever graced a classroom. To them I owe an incalculable debt, and I readily acknowledge their influence on my work.

During my fifty-plus years of ministry I have been able to acquire some of the best books ever to come from the pen of gifted giants. I have made use of them, and cited the sources of my information in the footnotes.

Special thanks must go to three individuals whose constant support and help has been of great encouragement to me: My wife, Aldyth, who critiqued each chapter as it was written; Maurice Bickley, whose expertise with computers was put to use in preparing the page-ready text for publication; and Dr. David Cahn whose painstaking correction of my literary gaffs greatly enhances the readability of my work. To them, and to the staff of Wipf and Stock Publishers, Inc., I say a very sincere *"Thank you!"*

As a "pigmy" I send this book forth to join my other books on the history of the Old Testament. May the One whom I serve use it to His glory and the edification of His people.

Cyril J. Barber.

CHAPTER ONE

THE MAKING OF A MAN OF GOD

PART ONE

Why should we concern ourselves with the life of Moses? Didn't he live too long ago for anything he did to be of value to us today? And isn't the same true of the book of Exodus? What does the freeing of the Israelites from bondage in Egypt have to do with us? If we have the New Testament, why do we need to immerse ourselves in the Old Testament?

In answering these questions we can do no better than reflect upon the words of the Apostle Paul when he wrote that *"All Scripture is inspired by God and profitable for teaching, for reproof, for correction, for training in righteousness; so that the man [and woman] of God may be adequate, equipped for every good work"* (2 Timothy 3:16). And let us not forget the words of Henry Wadsworth Longfellow, who reminded us that the "Lives of great men all remind us, we can make our lives sublime, and, departing, leave behind us, footsteps on the sands of time."

As far as the relevance of the book of Exodus is concerned, this portion of God's Word is of great importance to us, for it provides a necessary sequel to the history of the book of Genesis. The book of Genesis presents us with data from the beginning of creation to the end of the patriarchal age. Exodus describes how God's people were redeemed by one who was in many respects a leader like the Lord Jesus Christ, and constituted a nation (cf. Exodus 19:6; 32:10; Deuteronomy 4:8; 18:18-19).

Both the Old and New Testaments make frequent reference to the greatness of God in bringing His people out of Egypt (cf. Deuteronomy 4:34; 26:8), and the manner in which He constituted the sons of Jacob a nation (cf. Romans 3:1-2; 9:4-5; see also Psalm 147:19-20). The more we study the book of Exodus, therefore, the more we learn about God's holiness and His desire for His people to walk in the paths of righteousness.

Before we delve into the text of the second book of the Bible we must deal with a group of people who have caused some Bible scholars to misinterpret the context of the times. It has to do with the Hyksos,[1] commonly (though mistakenly) referred to as "the Shepherd Kings." They were "rulers of foreign lands"–a mixed, predominantly Northwest Semitic race that gradually infiltrated Egypt and finally took control (c. 1730-1570 B.C.).

The Hyksos did not assimilate with the Egyptians–a fact that in and of itself contains important lessons for us today. They ruled from their capital at Zoan-Tanis in the Delta, and were eventually expelled from Egypt by Ahmose

---

1. See Rawlinson, *History of Ancient Egypt*, I:111, 391; II:184-85; and regarding their expulsion from the land, II:200-202, 205-207. For recent confirmation of these facts, see C. F. Aling, *Egypt and Bible History: From the Earliest Times to 1000 B.C.* (Grand Rapids: Baker, 1981), 53-75.

I (1570-1546 B.C.). They erected temples to Baal, and there is evidence of their worship of the cult of the mother goddess. Their degrading practices may be seen in their devotion to such objects as nude figurines and serpents.

These people ruled *after* the time of Joseph and *before* the birth of Moses.

THE WOMEN WHOM GOD USED

The Midwives (Exodus 1:8-22)

Ahmose I is generally regarded as the "the new king who arose over Egypt, who did not know Joseph" (Exodus 1:8). He was succeeded by Amenhotep I (1546-1525 B.C.) who saw how the Israelites had multiplied and were continuing to spread over the land (Exodus 1:7). Fearing a repetition of the crisis precipitated by the Hyksos, he devised a means whereby the number of the Hebrews could be reduced.

Amenhotep I imposed harsh, forced labor on the Hebrews, but the more they were oppressed, the more they multiplied. The Egyptians took note of the failure of this plan and came to dread the Israelites. They continued to work them ruthlessly and made their lives bitter with hard labor in brick and mortar, and with all kinds of work in the fields. But this plan failed.

Amenhotep I was succeeded by Thutmose I who decided to kill off all new born baby boys. He told the Hebrew midwives, whose names were Shiphrah and Puah, "When you help the Hebrew women in childbirth and observe them on the delivery stool, if it is a boy, kill him; but if it is a girl, let her live."

The midwives, however, feared God and did not do what the king of Egypt had commanded.[2] In anger at the failure of his plan the king of Egypt summoned the midwives and demanded of them, "Why have you done this? Why have you let the boys live?"

The midwives answered Thutmose I, "Hebrew women are not like Egyptian women; they are vigorous and give birth before the midwives arrive."

This was an obvious lie,[3] and yet we read that God was good to the midwives and the people increased and became even more numerous than before. And because the midwives feared God, He established households for them and gave them families of their own.

---

2. P. G. Ryken, former senior pastor of the Tenth Presbyterian Church, Philadelphia, and now president of Wheaton College, IL, produced a massive commentary on the book of Exodus (Wheaton, IL: Crossway, 2005). On pages 40-44, has explains the "lie" told by the midwives, and cites several contemporary examples of such lies. It should be noted that in each of these instances those demanding the truth had usurped the place of God, and wanted information so that they could harm others.

Jochebed, the Mother of Moses (Exodus 2:1-4)

The account of the birth of Moses must, of necessity, begin with his parents. Amram (Exodus 6:20) was of the tribe of Levi long before God set this tribe apart to perform priestly functions. He married Jochebed (Numbers 26:59), his father's sister, and she bore to him Miriam and Aaron and Moses. Such marriages between members of the same family were permissible before the laws of consanguinity were established.

The parents of Moses lived in humble circumstances, for since the death of Joseph all the Israelites had descended to an almost dead level of uniformity. In their modest home the primary duties were undertaken by Jochebed, aided by Miriam as she grew older. Amram would have been forced to labor on whatever Pharaoh required, but may also have kept a small plot of ground where he cultivated seasonal

---

3. The lie told by the midwives and God's subsequent blessing of them has caused problems for conservative Christians. Scripture states emphatically that "*God desires truth in our inward parts*" (Psalm 51:6). How then can the Lord be good to the midwives and reward them for their deceit? It must be clearly understood that followers of Christ must be honest and truthful, with hearts open before the Lord; however, there are rare instances when people assume positions of authority and demand that we make confession to them. Only God is in possession of all the facts, and confession of wrong doing should be made to Him. Those who require more information than they have a right to receive plainly usurp His position of sovereignty. See G. Bush (1796-1859), *Notes ... On the Book of Exodus*, 2 vols. (Minneapolis: Klock and Klock, 1981), I:20, cols. *a* and *b*.

food-products to sustain his family. And, in time, he would have been assisted by Aaron who was but a toddler at the time of our story.

To the west, and visible from their lowly abode, was a vast necropolis (also known as the "City of the Dead") and the pyramids which were looked upon by the peasants as huge monuments to kingly vanity. They had been there when Abraham visited Egypt and seemed to defy time.

Aaron had been born before the Pharaonic edicts to exterminate the Hebrew boys at birth had been put into effect. Now, however, Pharaoh put into operation a new plan: All male children were to be thrown into the Nile River.[4]

It was at this time that Jochebed learned that she was soon to give birth to another child. She was painfully aware of Pharaoh's decree and perhaps prayed that this new infant would be a girl. But if another son was to be born to her, what could she and Amram do? How could she bear to have her baby's tender loving grasp torn from her breast, and allow him to be borne by uncaring hands to the bank of the Nile where he would either be suffocated by the cold waters or else have his life crushed out of him by the cruel jaws of a

---

4. It is possible that Amenhotep II based his decision on some perverted reasoning whereby he looked upon this form of infanticide as a gift to the Nile gods, Hapi and Khnum. See Herodotus, *History*, II:64; and E. A. Wallis Budge, *The Gods of the Egyptians*, 2 vols. (New York: Dover, 1969), I:286, 336; II:4, 155, 336.

crocodile? Such grief rent her heart until she felt that her anguish was more than she could bear.

As her pregnancy progressed Jochebed probably thought of various ways to save her child, should he be a boy; and perhaps she prayed to the God of Abraham, Isaac and Jacob for some form of divine intervention. She knew that faith must be linked with action, and so began to devise a plan to save her child's life.

In the course of time she delivered a boy,[5] and when she clasped him to her breast nothing in the world could have wrenched him from her. She felt thus nerved to defy the king and his myrmidons, and kept her son concealed. But what of their neighbors? Would they keep her secret? All oppressed cultures have their "informers," as the history of different wars plainly shows, and perhaps that is why at the end of three months Jochebed felt compelled to put into operation a desperate plan.

Hatshepsut, the Princess Who Adopted Moses (Exodus 2:5-10)

Jochebed knew of the plight of the princess Hatshepsut (see the **Introduction** to this volume), for she had been compelled to enter marriage with the intent of producing a male heir. Her efforts met only with failure, and her life as

---

5. In Exodus 2:2 Moses is described as "beautiful," in Acts 7:20 as "lovely, and in Hebrews 11:23 as "beautiful." Josephus, *Antiquities of the Jews*, II: 9: 4, adds to the biblical narrative some ideas of his own.

the wife of Thutmose II brought her only grief and unhappiness-so much so that her sorrow and distress had become widely known. At least one daughter had been born to her,[6] but this had only increased her desire for a son.

Jochebed also knew where Hatshepsut went to bathe in the Nile and so devised a plan. She would make a boat of bulrushes (i.e., of papyrus reeds),[7] thoroughly waterproof it, put her son in it, close the lid, and put it among the reeds near the place that Hatshepsut frequented.

Her plan worked! Hatshepsut saw the basket-like boat and sent one of her maids to fetch it. On opening it the baby began to cry, possibly because the sun's rays made him feel uncomfortable. She immediately discerned the truth behind his mother's bold move, and in that moment of time she decided to adopt Moses. And perhaps she thanked Isis[8] for giving her a son.

---

6. Philo, "Life of Moses", I: 4: 13-14, believes that the princess had been unable to have children, though a different tradition claims that she had borne two daughters.

7. For a modern illustration of this system of building reed boats, see Thor Hyerdahl's *The Ra Expeditions* (Garden City, NY: Doubleday, 1971); and the article in the *National Geographic* (January 1971), 44-71.

8. Isis, the wife of Osiris, was regarded as "she who could give the breath of life ...." See B. Watterson, *The Gods of Ancient Egypt* (New York: Facts on File, 1984), 61.

But there were problems to be worked out in the palace. How could she nurture her son, and at the same time explain her sudden conception of him to her husband?

It was at that moment that Miriam ran up to her with the suggestion that she go and find a Hebrew woman to nurse the baby for her.

Did Hatshepsut suspect that Miriam was part of Jochebed's plan? Did she discern the truth behind the drama that was being acted before her eyes? And when Miriam brought Jochebed to the princess did she sense in the Hebrew woman's eyes and the gentle way she took the baby from her that she was the child's mother?

Feigning indifference, Hatshepsut said, "Take this child away and nurse him *for me* and I shall give you your wages" (Exodus 2:9, emphasis added). And Jochebed did so. When Moses[9] had been weaned she took him to the palace and gave him to Hatshepsut. "And he became her son" (Exodus 2:10).

Something To Think About

There is much to learn from the example of the mid-wives, Jochebed and Hatshepsut:

---

9. The name given Moses has been variously explained. It seems likely that it came from the Egyptian root *mes* or *meses* which means "son of" or "child of," as in Aahmes, meaning "son of the moon," or Raamses, "child of the sun."

- The midwives illustrate for us the privilege of those in the helping professions. They never know when some baby whose life they save will grow up to achieve something truly great in his/her chosen profession.

- Jochebed probably weaned Moses at age three. Psychologists have shown that what a child learns in the first three years of his life determines the course of his life. It took time for the truths impressed upon Moses as a child to bear fruit, but in the end they did.

- In opposing the king's decree Hatshepsut shows us how even an unbelieving person can be the means in God's hands to cause the wrath of a powerful man to praise Him (cf. Psalm 76:10).

Two of God's promises are especially noticeable in these chapters. They are (1) The fulfillment of His word to make Israel a great nation (cf. Genesis 12:2; 17:20; 35:11; 46:3; Exodus 1:7); and (2) The faith of Moses' parents (Hebrews 11:23). He is faithful to His word!

Our attention is also drawn to some important facts: (1) The persecution of the Hebrews in Egypt prepared them to desire earnestly the freedom which is the natural desire of all people (and is true of those living in totalitarian cultures today). (2) The wicked desire power, and when they have it their decisions often ripen quickly into acts of the utmost cruelty (cf. Proverbs 28:12b, 15; 29:2b, 12). (3) A devout adherence to the will of God will not always deliver the righteous from persecution or death, but the way godly peo-

ple handle injustice can be a precious legacy to the generations that follow (See Romans 14:12).

CHAPTER TWO

THE MAKING OF A MAN OF GOD

PART TWO

Preparation in Egypt (2:1-15a)

Once in the palace Moses was given the finest education available, for Egypt was the most civilized and most advanced country in the world at that time. Education involved the mind as well as the body, and both fields were regarded as absolutely essential. Moses' training, therefore, involved a variety of games, gymnastics, and wrestling. It also included a game similar to the one described by Homer[10] in which one person threw a ball as high as he could, and the other, leaping up, caught the ball as it fell. This game required both strength and dexterity.

Stress was also placed on the development of the intellect. Young princes had to learn how to read and write, and these focused primarily on hieroglyphics and hieratic. Learning to read hieroglyphics was particularly difficult, probably extending over several years, and writing had to be done with the utmost care so that each picture or symbol represented distinct sounds or words or ideas, and could be differentiated from other similar figures. In addition Moses would also have learned mathematics (including fractions),

---

10. Homer, *Odyssey*, IX: 1, 374.

music (both vocal and instrumental), and poetry (cf. Deuteronomy 32).

At an early age Moses would have been taught at the palace by a pedagogue or tutor, but later on he would most likely have entered the university at Heliopolis (earlier known as the city of On), which was one of the great seats of learning and the principal center for the worship of the sun.[11] From this time onwards he added a knowledge of geometry, science, literature, philosophy, "epistolatory correspondence" (requiring a knowledge of Babylonian life and culture), astronomy and law[12] to what he had already learned.

Stephen summed up all these disciplines when he said that "Moses was educated in all the learning of the Egyptians, and was mighty in words ..." (Acts 7:22).

His university education concluded, Moses returned to the palace and resumed his position in Hatshepsut's household. And, perhaps, it was at this point in his life that he was given command of the Egyptian army and instructed to put down an uprising in Ethiopia. Those in Egypt did not believe that he would be successful. His enemies in the palace and among the priests hoped that he would be killed in

---

11. See the excellent description in A. P. Stanley's *Lectures on the History of the Jewish Church*, 3 vols. (London: Murray, 1875), I:73-76.
12. Herodotus, *History*, II:84 includes medicine in the list of the things Moses may have learned at the university of Heliopolis.

battle against the Ethiopians.[13]   In this they were disappointed. The victory he achieved demonstrated that he was also "mighty in deeds" (Acts 7:22).

But what of Hatshepsut?[14] Was she forced into exile during Moses' absence? Whatever the situation, when Moses returned to the palace he felt isolated. Gone now was his sense of belonging and worth that he had once enjoyed. And absent was the acclaim that he could have expected after achieving such a remarkable victory over Egypt's enemies.

These feelings of rejection were further exacerbated when he went to check on the welfare of the Hebrews. The story is well-known.   He saw an Egyptian flogging a Hebrew, and struck the Egyptian so forcefully that he killed him. Moses' action is not to be defended, for the Egyptian was hardly deserving of death. It is true that Moses, as a prince of Egypt, held an office that did not require him to hold a tribunal before passing sentence, but this hardly excuses his excessive use of force. The provocation was great, the motive was sympathy, and yet the act was hasty, passionate and self-willed.

---

13. Josephus, *Antiquities of the Jews*, II: 10:1-2. His expedition to Ethiopia is confirmed by Philo.

14. Tacit evidence for Hatshepsut's banishment and subsequent death may be deduced from the fact that when she died she was not laid to rest in her mortuary temple complex at Deir el-Bahri.

Having killed the Egyptian, Moses hid the body in the desert sand (Exodus 2:11-12). The next day he went out again. This time he saw two Hebrews fighting with one another. Again he intervened, only this time he received the harsh rebuttal, *"Who made you a prince or a judge over us?"* ...(Exodus 2:13-14; cf. Acts 7:35).

In addition to feelings of rejection, Moses now felt the humiliation that comes from it. He realized that Thutmose III would soon learn of what he had done and despatch members of the palace guard to have him arrested. He, therefore, either instructed a servant to saddle his horse or had his fastest chariot prepared for him. He then took off for the border, believing that the wisest course of action was for him to put as great a distance as possible between himself and the king.

Preparation in Midian (Exodus 2:15b–4:17)

Moses avoided the Egyptian outposts that had been established at strategic points throughout Saudi Arabia, and traveled with all speed southward down the Sinai peninsula. Then, turning eastward, he eventually came to Midian.

In Midian the proud, handsome, self-assured prince of Egypt entered a new university–the "university of hard knocks"--where he learned the lessons associated with failure, rejection, exile and loneliness.

The famous film maker, Cecil B. DeMille, dramatized for us Moses' arrival in Midian, though he omitted the fact that Moses was recognized as an Egyptian because he still wore the clothing and had the hairstyle of an Egyptian. Moses arrived at a well just as Jethro's daughters were about to water their father's sheep. When Moses saw a group of shepherds shoving them aside so that they could water their sheep first, he intervened. He quickly routed the shepherds, and then drew water for Jethro's sheep.

Harassment by the shepherds must have been a daily occurrence, for when Jethro's daughters returned to their father he asked them, "Why have you come back so soon today?" They replied, "An Egyptian delivered us from the hand of the shepherds, and even drew water for our flocks" (Exodus 2:18-19).

Jethro's next question reveals his kind and generous disposition: "Where is he then? Why have you left the man standing by the well? Invite him to have something to eat" (Exodus 2:20). And in accepting this friendly offer Moses began to experience the first feelings of acceptance and sense of worth that had been missing from his life.

Scripture passes over Jethro's invitation for Moses to stay with him. In the course of time he gave Moses his daughter Zipporah as his wife; and during the course of their marriage she bore him two sons, Gershom and Eliezer.

In naming his sons Moses gives us the only indications of the feelings that stirred his heart during his exile. At Gershom's birth Moses expressed his grief over being an exile, when he said, "I have been a stranger in a strange land" (Exodus 2:22). We do not know when his second son was born but Moses gave him the name of Eliezer, "My God has helped me." He is now at peace with his surroundings, and said, "For the God of my father is my helper, and has delivered me from the hand of Pharaoh" (Exodus 18:4).[15]

But nothing is said of the comfort that Zipporah brought him. When Dr. Charles Erdman was commenting on Exodus 4:24-25, he said of the marriage of Moses and Zipporah, "If this was romance, it was none the less pathetic. He whose companions had been courtiers, he who might have married some Egyptian princess, was now the husband of a simple shepherdess *who shared none of his culture, his tastes, his memories, or his dreams.*"[16]

Though Moses continued to shepherd his father-in-law's sheep for almost forty years, it must have been a humiliating task, for he was accustomed to the culture of Egypt, and the Egyptians abhorred sheep. In spite of this he endured the loneliness and learned how to care for and lead these wayward animals with their fleecy coats and propensity to wander off into dangerous places. And in the process of shepherding them he learned, albeit unconsciously, that people are much like sheep.

In addition, Moses also learned truths about himself. During the long days and lonely nights with no one to talk to, he came to know more about the One whom his parents and Jethro worshiped.[17]

---

15. Eliezer may not have been born for several years, for when the Lord sent Moses back to Egypt it would appear as if Eliezer was an infant.

16. C. R. Erdman, *The Book of Exodus* (Grand Rapids: Baker, 1982), 26, emphasis added.

Moses was nearing his eightieth year when, one day, while he was in a section of the desert that lay in the shadow of Mount Sinai (or Horeb), he was to be called to serve *Yahweh*, his God. It happened when he saw a burning bush– sometimes called the "thorn-tree of the desert," with its tangled branches and white thorns. The surprising thing was that this bush was not burned up. As he walked closer he heard a voice out of the bush calling him by name (Exodus 3:1-4).

The flame from the bush was in all probability a manifestation of the Shekinah glory, and the Angel of the Lord who spoke to him was none other than the Second Person of the Trinity (Exodus 3:2).

Moses showed his reverence for God by covering his face. The Lord then told Moses to remove his sandals because the place where he was standing was holy ground. With Moses' attention firmly established, the Lord then told him that He was aware of the suffering of the Israelites and intended to send him back to Egypt to lead them out of bondage (Exodus 3:7-10).

But Moses was not convinced that he was equal to the task. He shrank from the magnitude of the difficulties involved. His words, "Who am I, that I should go to Pharaoh ..." (Exodus 3:11) showed that he was no longer bold and impetuous. He was keenly aware of his imperfections and limitations.

---

17. A. P. Stanley has a good description of the kind of experience Moses may have had in his *Sinai and Palestine* (London: Murray, 1889), 67-68.

In answering Moses' objection the Lord said, "Certainly I will be with you," then to further reassure Moses of his call to be his nation's deliverer, He promised him that he would worship Him at this mountain (Exodus 3:12). In spite of this assurance Moses still felt himself unequal to the task, and so he raised another objection. "What if I do go to the sons of Israel and say to them 'The God of your fathers has sent me to you,' and they ask 'What is His name?' What shall I tell them?"

In the Old Testament "name" was synonymous with a person's character. In the case of God Himself His "*I AM WHO I AM*" (Exodus 3:14) indicated His absolute and essential being. It declared that He, as the Most High, is a person who is self-existent, changeless, and eternal, and the only One who is independent of everything and everyone else.

God further encouraged Moses by instructing him to speak to the elders of his people and assure them of the Lord's intent to lead them out of Egypt (Exodus 3:16-17). He also gave him certain signs to perform in the presence of the elders to accredit his person and mission. But He assured Moses that Pharaoh would not listen to him and so He would stretch out His hand and strike Egypt with different miracles (Exodus 3:19-20), so that in the end the Egyptians would beg the Hebrews to leave.

But Moses still was not convinced. He didn't feel competent to do all that the Lord was requiring of him, and, in Exodus 4:1-17, he listed his objections: "What if the people do not believe me" (4:1-9); "But I'm not eloquent, how can

I possibly convince people who do not want to be convinced?" (4:10-12); "Lord, I'm not sure I'm the right man for the job. Please send someone else" (4:13). At this, God became angry and told him that at that precise moment Aaron was coming to meet him, and that he would be his spokesman (4:14-17).

The Lord answered each of these objections and further assured Moses that "all the men who formerly sought to kill him were dead" (Exodus 4:19).

Having no more excuses to make to the Lord, Moses returned to Jethro and asked to be allowed to go and see the members of his extended family who were still in Egypt. Permission was given, and taking his wife and sons Moses mounted them on a donkey[18] and set out for the land beyond the Nile. En route he became so ill he believed he was soon to die (Exodus 4:24ff). He then realized that he had put off circumcising his younger son (perhaps at the insistence of Zipporah). His neglect placed Eliezer outside the Covenant that the Lord had instituted with Abraham. Dr. Charles C. Ryrie is of the opinion that Moses' failure was designed to teach him that disobeying God and incurring His wrath was more serious than anything that could befall him at the hands of the new Pharaoh.[19]

---

18. The singular "donkey" (Exodus 4:20) is probably a Hebraism for more animals of the same kind. In all probability the small caravan consisted of three of four donkeys with Moses leading the way.
19. See the valuable notes in the *Ryrie Study Bible*, New American Standard Version (Chicago: Moody, 1995), 96.

At Moses' insistence Zipporah took a flint knife and circumcised Eliezer (Exodus 4:25-26a). She then threw the foreskin at Moses' feet, and exclaimed scornfully, "You are a bridegroom of blood to me."[20] Moses apparently realized that his wife would not support him in his mission, and so sent her back to her father. They were later reunited when he led the Israelites out of Egypt (cf. Exodus 18:2-3), but there is no indication that Zipporah had changed.

Soon after his separation from Zipporah, Moses met Aaron. We can only imagine their glad reunion, the questions they asked about each other's family, and the difficulties of the task before them. And together they made their way to Egypt.

Something to Think About

As we consider the way in which the Lord prepared Moses for the difficult task of leading His people to freedom we come to realize that He was then, and still is aware of the suffering of His own. He was also aware of the unbelief of the leaders of His people, and so He gave Moses signs to convince them of the truth of his words. And He assured Moses of eventual victory in spite of the obstinacy of Pharaoh (Exodus 4:21ff.). It is the same today.

---

20. There is no evidence that Zipporah was a God-fearer like her father or her husband. She objected to the rite of circumcision even though it had been instituted by God with Abraham, and even when she relented it was with ill-grace, and she showed her anger against her husband by her actions.

We also note God's patience in dealing with Moses (and, as a concession, sending Aaron to help him). In much the same way He is patient with us, even when we stubbornly refuse to heed the teaching of His Word. And in grace He has given us the Holy Spirit to indwell us and be our Helper.

In addition, and as a warning, we note that there is no evidence in the text that Zipporah shared her husband's faith or sense of calling. The same is true of many Christian marriages today. What a tragedy for someone who is stubborn or an unbeliever to pass from this life and have to give an account to the Lord of one's wasted opportunities.

George Macdonald (1824-1905) wrote of his experience when he, like Moses, wrestled with God about his call to service.

I said–"Let me walk in the fields."
  He said–"No, walk in the town."
I said--"There are no flowers there."
  He said–"No flowers, but a crown."
I said–"But the skies are dark;
  There is nothing but noise and din."
And He wept as He sent me back–
  "There is more," He said, "there is sin."
I said–"I shall miss the light
  And the friends will miss me, they say."
He answered, "Choose to-night
  If I am to miss you, or they."

I pleaded for time to be given.
  He said—"Is it hard to decide?
  It will not be hard in Heaven
  To have followed the steps of your Guide."
Then into His hand went mine,
  And into my heart came He,
  And I walked in a light divine
  The path I had feared to see.

CHAPTER THREE

PRELUDE TO THE TEN PLAGUES

The *Oxford American Dictionary* defines "prelude" in part as "an action or event that precedes another and leads up to it...." In this respect Exodus 4:21-23 is a prelude to God's mighty miracles by which Pharaoh Amenhotep II (1450-1423)[21] finally let the Israelites go. But how was God's plan to be carried out? The instrument he used was Moses who first requested that God's people be allowed to go out into the desert and worship Him, but when this request was denied, it later became a demand. With each refusal on Pharaoh's part the inevitable confrontation became an unavoidable reality.

En Route to Egypt (Exodus 4:27-31)

In this section we see Moses as a lone wanderer. He has recently recovered from what could have been a terminal illness. Now, as we follow him we see him treading his way through the desolate wadis of the Sinai peninsula. He is intent on intercepting his brother. Ironically, the route he now takes is the reverse of the one he had taken forty years earlier when, in the full bloom of mature manhood, he had fled from Egypt with no fixed destination in mind.

---

21. Thutmose III (1482-1450), the pharaoh of the oppression, was dead (Exodus 2:23-25; 4:19). See J. Rea, *Bulletin of the Evangelical Theological Society* (III, #3, 1960), 58-69.

The words the Lord had spoken to Moses are important if we are to correctly understand God's dealings with Amenhotep. The Lord had said to Moses, "When you go back to Egypt ... you shall say to Pharaoh, *'Thus says Yahweh, the God of the Israelites, Israel is My son, My firstborn. Let My son go that he may serve Me'....*"

The position of the firstborn son in a family is best described by Jacob. Speaking directly to Reuben, he said, "You are my firstborn; my might and the beginning of my strength; ..." (Genesis 49:3).

The firstborn son held a special place of honor in the family.[22] His position of privilege was later expanded to include the *nation* of Israel, and that is how the word "firstborn" is used in this passage. So, when *Yahweh*, the covenant-keeping God of the Israelites, said to Pharaoh, "Israel is My son, My firstborn," he was justified in demanding that Pharaoh let His people go. Of course, to refuse such a legitimate request would bring dire consequences on the one turning a deaf ear to such an entreaty.

Now, as Moses went to meet his brother, Aaron, his spirits were buoyed. He hadn't seen him for forty years. What changes might he expect? But he also was saddened by the circumstances that had made it necessary to send Zipporah and their sons back to her father.[23] The angst that he probably felt would have weighed heavily upon him. But laying aside these personal feelings he trod the sandy waste,

---

22. This blessing extends to believers, see Romans 8:29-30 and Hebrews 12:23.

trying as best he could to protect himself from the fierce rays of the sun.

When the brothers saw each other they probably ran to meet one another. What changes had the past forty years made? Were they both grey? And what marks of servitude had been left on Aaron's body? All we know for certain is that Moses retained his vigor, and would do so for another forty years (cf. Deuteronomy 34:7).[24]

Moses and Aaron had much to talk about. Moses would have wanted to know if his parents, Amram and Jochebed, were still alive. And what of Miriam; had she finally married Ham?[25]

Moses would have told Aaron about Jethro, his marriage to Zipporah, and their two sons, Gershom and Eliezer; and Aaron would have told Moses about his wife Elizabeth and their children: Nadab and Abihu, and Eleazar and Ith-

---

23. Rawlinson, *Moses*, 82, wrote: "Zipporah had scarcely shown herself to be a 'helpmate.' If her abhorrence of the rite of circumcision had caused it to be delayed, she had brought her husband into imminent danger. When she relented, it was with an ill grace, with an unseemly act, and with words that showed her anger against her husband, if not positive dislike of him."

24. Diodorus Sicilus (XXXIV: 1) provides a colorful description of both men.

25. According to Josephus (*Antiquities of the Jews*, 3:2, 4; and 6, 1), Miriam was married to the famous Hur, and, through him, was the grandmother of the architect Bezaleel.

amar. Then each would have recounted God's providential care of them in spite of the hardships they had endured.

Moses would also have told Aaron all that the Lord God had said to him, and the signs that He had commanded him to perform (Exodus 4:28). This done, they went on their way to Egypt together where they convened a meeting with the elders of their people.

Though Scripture records one fact upon another as if they were almost simultaneous, it probably took time for the elders to assemble, for they would have been living in different parts of Egypt. Only when they were all together could Aaron "speak to them all the words that *Yahweh*, their God, had spoken to Moses." Significantly, they believed him and bowed down and worshiped (Exodus 4:30-32).

Face to Face With Pharaoh (5:1-7)

But who was Amenhotep II who occupied the throne of Egypt? He believed that he was the visible god on earth. In his mind no pure monotheism could for a moment be compared with his divine exaltation.[26] After all, he occupied the throne of the god Horus, and was himself the "giver of life." And among the accolades by which he was known was "the good god," and "son of the sun." And to his credit he had enlarged the priestly city of Heliopolis (earlier known as On) and proclaimed himself "Divine Ruler of Heliopolis"!

---

26. Stanley, Sinai and Palestine, xxxvi.

Who then dared challenge his authority?

Though Amenhotep II had engaged in three military expeditions in Asia (in his 3rd, 7th, and 9th years), he was in reality a weak king, readily claiming for himself the achievements of others. He was also capricious, vain, and vengeful.[27] It took courage for Moses and Aaron to confront such a self-opinionated man,[28] with his courtiers fawning over him and his soldiers ready to remove from his presence any who might anger him.

Now imagine the scene as Moses and Aaron appeared before his throne. Their request was clearly stated. "Thus says Yahweh,[29] the God of Israel, 'Let My people go that they may celebrate a feast to me in the wilderness.'" (Exodus 5:1).

His reply reveals how arrogant, self-willed and despotic he had become: "Who is this Yahweh that I should obey His

---

27. Eusebius (c. A.D. 264-339), *Preparation for the Gospel*, trans. E. H. Gifford (Grand Rapids, 1981), ix:27.
28. During this period Egypt maintained two capitals, the one in Thebes and the other in Memphis. It would have been easy for Moses and Aaron to confront Amenhotep II while he was in Memphis. See W. C. Hayes, *The Scepter of Egypt* 2 vols. (Cambridge, MA: Harvard U. P., 1959), II:141.
29. Considerable debate has existed over how much the Israelites knew of the Divine Name, *Yahweh*. A helpful discussion is to be found in *Unger's Old Testament Commentary*, 110, col. a. See also R. D. Wilson, *Princeton Theological Review* (1924), 108-119.

voice to let Israel go? I do not know [this god] , and besides I will not let Israel go" (Exodus 5:2).

Moses and Aaron were then in all probability ushered out of Amenhotep's throne room so that the next petitioner could be shown in. They bided their time and, perhaps when the last petitioner had gone his way, they again sought an audience with Pharaoh. Their request was brief, "The God of the Hebrews has met with us. Now let us take a three-day journey into the desert to offer sacrifices to *Yahweh* our God, or He may strike us with plagues or with the sword" (Exodus 5:3).

At best, Amenhotep was a self-absorbed dictator; at worst he was a cold, malicious tyrant. He could be benign when it suited him or merciless when provoked. He again refused to accede to Moses and Aaron's request, and based his refusal (as far as he was concerned) on two grounds: (1) The God whose demands were reported to him, was not his God, and had no authority over him; and (2) He needed the Israelites to work on his building projects (Exodus 5:4).

Thereupon Moses and Aaron were rudely dismissed.

That same day Pharaoh commanded the taskmasters over the Israelites, saying, "You shall no longer give the people straw to make bricks as before. Let them go and gather straw for themselves. And you shall lay on them the quota of bricks which they made before. You shall not reduce it. For they are idle; therefore they cry out, saying, 'Let us go and sacrifice to our God.' Let more work be laid on the men, that they may labor in it, and let them not regard false words" (Exodus 5:7-9).

Pharaoh's refusal to give them straw made their work doubly hard. The taskmasters and their officers went out and spoke to the people, saying, "Thus says Pharaoh: 'I will not give you straw. Go, get yourselves straw where you can find it; yet none of your work will be reduced.'" So the people were scattered abroad throughout all the land of Egypt to gather stubble instead of straw. Also, the officers of the children of Israel, whom Pharaoh's taskmasters had set over them, were beaten and were asked, "Why have you not fulfilled your task in making brick both yesterday and today, as before?" (cf. Exodus 5:6-14).

Labor as hard as they might, the brickmakers could not produce their full quota, with the result that they were beaten relentlessly. The foremen then came to Pharaoh and pleaded with him for straw to help them make the bricks, but he refused. His response was, "You are lazy, that's what you are, lazy! That is why you keep saying, 'Let us go and sacrifice to Yahweh.' Now get to work. You will not be given any straw, yet you must produce your full quota of bricks."[30]

On leaving the palace, the Israelites who had been there to intercede before Pharaoh encountered Moses and Aaron.

---

30. There is archaeological evidence that some cities built by the Israelites had bricks made of straw at the lower level, but no straw in the bricks used as the city neared its completion. See C. F. Nims, *The Biblical Archaeologist*, XIII, 2 (1950), 22-28.

Their angry words to the Lord's servants reveal their deep
frustration and resentment. They said, in effect, "Now look
what you've done. Your interference has made our lives
more difficult. You've succeeded in arousing the ire of Pharaoh, and you have caused the entire nation to stink in his
nostrils."

These words struck deep into the hearts of Moses and
Aaron, and in despair Moses prayed to the Lord (Exodus
5:22-23). Many men and women of God have similarly
turned to the Lord when circumstances seemed blackest and
hope had all but faded from their lives. The precedent set by
Moses is one we all should follow (cf. Psalm 11). And in
response, the Lord said to him, "Now you shall see what I
will do to Pharaoh; for under compulsion he will let them
go, and under compulsion he will drive them out of his
land" (Exodus 6:1).

By way of further encouragement, God said, "I am *Yahweh*, and I appeared to Abraham, Isaac, and Jacob, as *El
Shaddai*, (God Almighty), but by My name *Yahweh* I did
not make Myself known to them.[31] I also established My
covenant with them, to give them the land of Canaan, the
land in which they sojourned. And now, I have heard the
groaning of the sons of Israel, because the Egyptians are
holding them in bondage, and I have remembered My covenant. Say, therefore, to the sons of Israel, 'I am *Yahweh*, and
I will bring you out from under the burdens of the Egyptians, and I will deliver you from their bondage. I will also

---

31. The patriarchs were familiar with the name *Yahweh*, but
    they did not understand its significance.

redeem you with an outstretched arm and with great judgments. Then I will take you for My people, and I will be your God; and you shall know that I am *Yahweh* your God, who brought you out from under the burdens of the Egyptians. I will bring you to the land which I swore to give to Abraham, Isaac, and Jacob, and I will give it to you for a possession; I am *Yahweh*"–The all-powerful, covenant-keeping God (Exodus 6:1-8).

The Lord then gave Moses and Aaron a charge to deliver to the Israelites, but the people did not listen to Moses on account of their despondency over their cruel bondage (Exodus 6:9). Nor is it surprising that Moses shrank from conveying the same message to Pharaoh. The next time they met it was not with a request for a three-day journey into the desert within the limits of Egypt, but a demand that he allow them to go out of his land.

Clearly, a "line has been drawn." The issue had been clearly defined. It was a contest between Pharaoh and Yahweh. A command had been issued by the eternal God who had come to answer the tears and groans of His people who were being abused and exploited by a tyrant.

But what are we to make of Exodus 6·14-27? The inclusion of the list of the "heads of the fathers' households" is unexpected. An older generation of Bible critics believed that this historic record was inserted by an editor who had the material and did not know what to do with it, so he inserted it here. But this does great disservice to the Holy Spirit who inspired this record (2 Timothy 3:16). In accordance with the literary norms of the day, before an account

of some great exploit could be given, readers were informed
of the noble character of the participants. And this is what
we have here.

With the "battle lines" clearly drawn, the Lord now said
to Moses, *"See, I make you as* **Elohim** *(God) to Pharaoh,
and your brother Aaron shall be your prophet. You shall
speak all that I command you, and your brother Aaron shall
speak to Pharaoh that he let the sons of Israel go out of his
land. But I will harden Pharaoh's heart that I may multiply
My signs and My wonders in the land of Egypt. When Pharaoh does not listen to you, then I will lay My hand on Egypt
and bring out My hosts, My people the sons of Israel, from
the land of Egypt by great judgments. The Egyptians shall
know that I am Yahweh, when I stretch out My hand on
Egypt and bring out the sons of Israel from their midst"*
(Exodus 7:1-5).[32]

The means by which the Lord would accomplish His
purpose for His people would be through the hardening of
Pharaoh's heart. Pharaoh had already demonstrated his
obstinacy, and he would now experience a judicial hardening of his heart against Moses, the Israelites, and God Himself.

---

32. God made Moses His theocratic representative to Pharaoh.
Whatever was said or done to Moses was looked upon as
having been said and done to God Himself. For an excellent
discussion of the theocracy, see Pentecost, *Things to Come*,
433ff.

The demonstration of God's power would be through signs, wonders, and great judgments. In the end even the Egyptians would come to realize the power and authority of Israel's God.

Exodus 7:7 concludes with this brief statement about Moses and Aaron: "And Moses was eighty years old and Aaron eighty-three years old when they spoke to Pharaoh."

Something to Think About

1. As we look back over these chapters we note God's assurance of absolute victory in spite of diverse obstacles.

2. In the case of Zipporah (and men and women who are like her) we consider the unimaginable loss which accompanies their failure to appreciate spiritual realities because the focus of their life is on the personal/temporal.

3. Note the names used to describe who God is (e.g., *Yahweh.*, 6:2-3, 6; El Shaddai, 6:3; His past work, 6:4-5; His present plan 6:6-7; the nation's future prospects, 6:8). What encouragement can we derive from these intimations of what God is like?

4. It is also important to note that the hardening of Pharaoh's heart (6:3) was the result of disobedience to God's appeal for His people to be released. Throughout Scripture a "hard heart" always refers to at a person who is in rebellion against God.

5. One person known only as "J. H. S." penned the following words of encouragement:

   O God of the impossible!
       Since all things are to You
   But soil in which Omnipotence
       Can work mightily,

   Each trial may make us become
       The means that will display
   How o'er what seems impossible
       Our God has perfect sway.

   The things that are to us so hard,
       The foes that are so strong,
   Are just the very ones that may
       Awake a triumph song.

   O God of the impossible
       When we no hope can see,
   Grant us the faith that still believes
       All is possible to You![33]

---

33. Full credit will be given the author in a later printing of
this work, if suitable data can be obtained.

CHAPTER FOUR

SIGNS AND WONDERS

IN THE LAND OF HAM[34]

PART ONE

Have you pondered the connection between Moses' despair at his rejection by the people (Exodus 5:21) and God's encouragement of him (Exodus 6:1-13, noting esp. 6:9)? His mission to Pharaoh had ended in failure. His high hopes for his peoples' liberation had resulted in defeat. To say that he was discouraged is to put it mildly. But after prayer the Lord clarified the issues for his beleaguered servant. God's plan was far broader than anything Moses had imagined. The battle lines had been clearly drawn. The contest was now between Pharaoh and the Lord.

In the next few chapters the events leading up to the departure of the Israelites from the land are sketched in the form of specific signs and judgments. "Signs" verified the credentials of Moses, and "judgments" were intended by God to punish Pharaoh for his continued subjucation of His people.

---

34. The title of this chapter is taken from Deuteronomy 6:22, Nehemiah 9:10, and Jeremiah 32:20.

The Second Meeting with Pharaoh (Exodus 7:8-13)

After encouraging his despondent servant, the Lord sent Moses and Aaron back to Pharaoh. They were instructed to meet with him as the rose-red fingers of Ra, the sun god, were pushing back the shades of night. Apparently Pharaoh made regular sacrifices to Hapi (the spirit of the Nile) and Khnum (the guardian of the Nile).[35]

It would have been natural for Pharaoh to ask for the credentials of *Yahweh's* ambassadors, but his pride would not allow him to stoop so low. We do know that when the brothers stood before him Aaron threw his staff on the ground and it became a snake. Pharaoh may have been marginally impressed by what he saw, but when his wise men and sorcerers and magicians did the same, his attitude changed.

The question may be validly asked, How were the magicians able to counterfeit the miracle performed by Moses and Aaron? Answers run the gamut from demonic involvement to quickly substituting snakes for their wooden staffs. Then there is also the possibility that they placed their snakes in some form of cataleptic state from which they awoke when thrown on to the ground. The fact that Aaron's snake ate up the snakes of the magicians did not impress Pharaoh, and he became more resistant to God's

---

35. See E. A. Wallis Budge, *The God's of the Egyptians*, I:198; II:77, 129; Watterson, *The God's of Ancient Egypt*, 28-31. See also the "Hymn to the Nile," *Ancient Near Eastern Texts*, 372-73.

will.[36] We are not surprised, therefore, that he would not listen to Moses and Aaron.

Readers of some versions of the Bible are confused over how a righteous, loving God could harden Pharaoh's heart. The answer is relatively simple. Pharaoh was unwilling to obey God, and with every new appeal he became more stubborn and defiant. In other words, he hardened his own heart. In the end God judicially punished him for continuously resisting His will.

---

36. The NIV uses the term "unyielding" to describe Pharaoh's attitude. Three different Hebrew words are used to account for the hardening of Pharaoh's heart. The first is *kabed*, meaning "to be heavy, insensitive, dull" (Exodus 7:14; 8:15, 32; 9:7, 34). The second is *qasah*, and implies that which is "hard, severe, or fierce" (cf. Exodus 7:3; 13:15). The third is *hazaq*, and conveys the idea of "growing or becoming strong, rigid, hard, unmovable." In 7:13 *hazaq* is used in the perfect tense indicating completed action. In other words Pharaoh's heart was not simply becoming hard, it was already inflexible!

The fact that Pharaoh refused to yield to the evidence presented by Moses and Aaron is evident from Exodus 7:13, 14, 22; 8:15, 19, 32; 9:7, 34-35; 13:15. His intransigence blinded his eyes and brought upon him God's judicial wrath (cf. Exodus 4:21; 7:3; 9:12; 10:1, 20, 27; 11:10; 14:4, 8, 17).

To accurately understand the nuances of the original text readers are urged to use a modern, literal translation like the *New American Standard Bible*.

AN ANALYSIS OF THE PLAGUES

There is a symmetry to these plagues/judgments.[37] Numbers 1 through 3 form a group, numbers 4, 5 and 6 constitute a second group, and numbers 7 through 9 make up a third group. The tenth plague/judgment stands alone.

It is interesting to notice in each of the groups that the first and second judgments are announced to Pharaoh before they take place. Morning was the time when the first was proclaimed to Pharaoh, and the place was the river bank. The second was made known to Pharaoh in the palace, but the third judgment began without warning. Furthermore, as the judgments continued they increased in severity.[38]

The first two miracles performed by Moses and Aaron were counterfeited by Pharaoh's magicians,[39] but when the dust was turned to lice they were forced to acknowledge "This is the finger of God" (Exodus 8:19).

---

37. The signs and wonders that we read about in Exodus 7:14–10:27 are commonly referred to as "plagues," but they were in reality *judgments*–the judgments of God against the gods of Egypt and the sins of Pharaoh (see Numbers 33:4b). It is estimated that the Egyptians worshiped at least eighty gods. The judgments God sent were designed to show the impotence of these deities and the futility of the Egyptians' misguided devotion.
38. See the Australian magazine, *Buried History* (September, 1967), 17.
39. The two most prominent ones were named Jannes and Jambres, see 2 Timothy 3:8-9.

In the second group of judgments a distinction is drawn between the Israelites and the Egyptians, for from this time on only the Egyptians were affected and those living in Goshen were exempt. These judgments, as well as those in group 3, were effected either by the hand or the staff of Moses or Aaron.

The miraculous nature of these judgments is clearly seen when we compare Exodus 8:3; 9:5, 18; and 10:4. Furthermore, the flashback given in Exodus 12:12, where the Lord stated: *"Against all the gods of Egypt I will execute judgment,"* makes everything plain.

When casual readers review these judgments they often accuse God of being capricious. The late Dr. Joseph Free, for many years professor of Archaeology, Wheaton College, IL, analyzed His actions as follows. There was ...

- *Intensification.* The frogs, insects, murrain, hail, and darkness were all known in Egypt,   but in these judgments what God did was intensified far beyond ordinary occurrence.
- *Prediction.* The precise time was set for the coming of the flies (8:23), murrain (9:5), hail   (9:18), and locusts (10:4). And the removal time was also set: frogs (8:10), thunder   (9:29).
- *Discrimination.* In Goshen there were no flying insects (8:22), murrain (9:4), or hail (9:26), et cetera.
- *Orderliness.* The severity of the judgments increased until they ended with the death of Pharaoh's first-born.

- *Moral purpose.* These judgments were not freaks of nature, but aimed at discrediting the   gods of Egypt.[40]

A variety of natural explanations has been given to account for these judgments. One of the most interesting was advanced by Angelos G. Galanopolus of the Seizmological Institute in Athens.[41] He connected the events that took place in Egypt with the eruption of the volcano on the island of Thera (Santorini) that took place in around 1400 B.C. This eruption was many times more powerful than the 1883 expulsion of lava and gas that blew the top off the 1460-foot high volcano Krakatoa, sending a fiery column of dust 33 miles into the air and hurled rocks 50 miles away. Dust circled the earth, turning sunsets red. And when the volcano collapsed into the 600-foot deep crater in the sea, it created tidal waves which destroyed 295 towns and sent 36,000 people to a watery grave.

According to geologists who have worked with Galanopolus' theory the explosion of Thera (Santorini) must have been many times more violent than Krakatoa. It is conjectured, therefore, that this cataclysmic eruption that took place in the middle of the Mediterranean could easily have accounted for natural phenomena that resulted in the plagues of Egypt.[42]   But no amount of literary skill can

---

40. Free, *Archaeology and Bible History*, 95.
41. His work carries the title *Seismike geographica tes Hellados* (1955).

account for the death of all the first-born in Egypt on the night preceding the expulsion of the Israelites from the "land of the Nile."

Galanopolus' theory provides an ingenious explanation for the events that prompted the Exodus, and it also supports the early date of circa 1400. There are a few snags with this view, however, and one of the foremost concerns the length of time the effects of the eruption on Thera (Santorini) lasted. God's judgments on the Egyptians probably began in the Hebrew month of Ab (July-August) when the Nile flooded its banks, and they continued until Passover the next year (a period of approximately nine months).

The First Judgment : The Water of the Nile Turned to Blood (Exodus 7:14-25)

In the first judgment the water of the Nile was turned to blood (Exodus 7:14-21). It would appear as if Pharaoh came early in the morning to pay his devotion to the gods Hapi and Khnum. The river was the sole source of drinking water for the country, and was regarded as the life-blood of its people.

By turning the water of the Nile to blood both Hapi, the god of the Nile, and Osiris, the god of water, were shown to be impotent. The fish, that were an integral part of the peo-

---

42. I. Wilson, *Exodus, the True Story* (New York: Harper & Row, 1986), 97-114, and for the plagues of Egypt, 115-27. For a different view see W. M. Flinders Petrie, *Egypt and Israel* (London: SPCK, 1911), 35-36.

ples' diet died, and this discredited the goddess Hat-Mehyt, whose symbol was a fish.[43]

By using their secret arts the Egyptian magicians did the same thing, and Pharaoh's heart became so resistant to the evidence presented to him that he would not listen to Moses and Aaron. Instead, he turned away from them and went into his palace, refusing to take this dramatic sign to heart. To survive, all the Egyptians and those living in Goshen dug along the Nile bank to get drinking water, because they could not drink water from the river (Exodus 7:22-24).[44]

---

43. Watterson, *The Gods of Ancient Egypt*, 73.
44. Pharaoh was sworn to defend the truth. In Egyptian theology the "heart" was the essence of the person, that is why in the Egyptian *Book of the Dead*, the heart was weighed to determine if the deceased was worthy of eternal life. If Pharaoh had realized how hard his heart had become and the awful fate that awaited him he would have trembled before Moses and Aaron and asked for forgiveness.

   The Book of the Dead which was found in the Palace of Anubis, describes how the heart of Ani, the scribe, was weighed against the feather of righteousness (see Plates XXXI and XXXII in the British Museum). If it was found that his heart was too heavy, he would be condemned for his sins and thrown to a voracious monster. The full text of *The Book of the Dead* was published in New York by Bell Publishing Company.

The Second Judgment: Frogs (Exodus 8:1-15)

The second judgment came seven days later and focused on the frog goddess Heqt (also spelled Heka) who was responsible for fertility. She was also the patroness of midwives, and is presented in Egyptian paintings with the body of a woman and the head of a frog.[45]

When the annual flood waters of the Nile receded, it was common for frogs to spawn in the marshes that lined the river bank. At this time of year the Nile had not begun to retreat and so the activity of the frogs was most unusual. They took over everything; and similar stories, told by Diodorus Sicilus (*Works*, iii:30) and Pliny (*Natural History*, viii:29), relate how these infestations forced the inhabitants of certain regions to leave their homes and find a place to live elsewhere.

Apparently in Egypt the frogs from the Nile were not merely an annoyance, but were disgusting in appearance. And to have these loathsome reptiles with their cold, rough skin in ones' home and kitchen, bedroom and upon one's bed, was intolerable. And when they died in large numbers and were swept into heaps in the streets, their stench became unbearable.

Once again Pharaoh told Moses and Aaron that he would let the Israelites go, but when the frogs were removed, he changed his mind (cf. Exodus 8:8 and15). His failure to honor his word provoked the Lord and He sent

---

45. See Budge, *The Gods of the Egyptians*, II:378-79 (#6).

upon Egypt, without any previous warning, another judgment.

The Third Judgment: Fleas/Lice (Exodus 8:16-19).

The Egyptians were fastidious about their personal habits. They bathed twice a day, with the priests bathing twice as often. Their bodies were also shaved every second day. Imagine their horror when the very dust of the streets seemed to breed lice or fleas that crawled up their legs and covered their bodies leaving painful welts that itched and caused intense discomfort.

Not only were the bodies of the priests affected, but these parasitic insects were also found on their sacred animals, including the Apis bull. The animals worshiped by the Egyptians were kept with scrupulous care and bathed so that they might win the god's favor. Such an affliction upon the sacred beasts would have caused the Egyptians to suspect that they had been deserted by their deities. This invasion also showed the powerlessness of Pharaoh, the embodiment of the gods, and led them to the conclusion that they had nothing to expect but ruin, for the balance of *ma'at* (universal equilibrium that Pharaoh was supposed to maintain) had been disrupted.

In this connection an interesting story illustrating Pharaoh's powerlessness is told by H. J. L. Beadnell, an archaeologist and historian, who spent many years in Egypt. He relates how one day he was sitting in the shade of some bushes when he noticed that the sand appeared to be moving. Closer inspection revealed the fact that the surface of the ground was a moving mass of minute fleas or lice, and at that moment thousands of them were crawling up his legs. He took a closer look at these parasites and found that they were almost invisible, being no larger than finely crushed grains of pepper. He beat a hasty retreat to the place where he was staying, and as he did so pondered the words of Scripture, *"the dust of the land became lice throughout all the land of Egypt."*

The magicians admitted that they could not duplicate what Moses and Aaron had done, and confessed that what Pharaoh now saw was nothing less than "the finger of God."[46] But Pharaoh remained obdurate, and he would not listen to them.

Something to Think About

Pharaoh illustrates for us how deliberate, wilful sin hardens the heart, and the more it is indulged the more difficult it becomes for a person—man or woman—to break free from its grip. Closely associated with this is the terrible power men and women have to resist the will of God and inflicting pain and suffering on others.

What confidence can we derive from the fact that while God permitted the Egyptian magicians to imitate what Moses and Aaron did, His superiority is clearly shown in the outcome?

---

46. "The finger of God" refers to His special work or power, by which He seems to perform mighty acts effortlessly.

We should also note the power of Satan to deceive people with counterfeits of the truth (cf. 1 Timothy 4:1-2; 2 John 7)–something that will become prevalent "in the last days" (cf. Mark 13:22; 2 Thessalonians 2:9-10; and Revelation 16:3-7). How may we guard against being seduced by these "lying wonders"?

Amenhotep's pride and arrogance were such that he refused to even consider that the God of the Israelites had a right to rule His peoples' worship and service. He reminds us of another Egyptian monarch whom Percy Bysshe Shelley wrote about in his poem Ozymandias.

I met a traveller from an antique land
Who said: "Two vast and trunkless legs of stone
Stand in the desert. Near them on the sand,
Half sunk, a shattered visage lies, whose frown,
And wrinkled lip, and sneer of cold command,
Tell that its sculptor well those passions read
Which yet survive, stamped on these lifeless things,
The hand that mocked them and the heart that fed.
And on the pedestal these words appear–
  "My name is Ozymandias, king of kings:
  Look on my works, ye Mighty, and despair!"
Nothing besides remains. Round the decay
Of that colossal wreck, boundless and bare
The lone and level sands stretch far away.[47]

---

47. *The Complete Works of Shelley*, ed. G. E. Woodberry (Boston: Houghton, Mifflin, 1901), 356.

Solomon spoke the truth when he said, "Pride goes before destruction, and an arrogant spirit before a fall" (cf. Proverbs 16:18).

CHAPTER FIVE

SIGNS AND WONDERS

IN THE LAND OF HAM

PART TWO

One strategy used by despots to break the spirit of people who either ask for a favor or desire some leniency is to promise that they will consider their request or (in the case of the Israelites) accede to their wishes, only to go back on their word (cf. Exodus 8:8, 15). And this may have been a strategy Pharaoh attempted.

We are not told how many days elapsed between the third and fourth judgments, but the interval may have given Pharaoh reason to believe that his plan of promise-and-withdrawal had worked.

The Fourth Judgment: Flying Insects
(Exodus 8:20-32)

Knowing Pharaoh's habits, *Yahweh* instructed Moses to rise early in the morning and go to the place where Pharaoh came down to the Nile, and say to him: "This is what *Yahweh* says, 'Let My people go, that they may serve Me.'"

It is easy to understand why Pharaoh would prefer the early morning to go and pay homage to the god of the Nile, for the air was cool and the opal tints that heralded the rising of Ra from his nightly slumber had not yet given way before his awesome (and, dare we say, oppressive) majesty. The bitterness of the previous judgment had passed, and Pharaoh now looked forward to a time of peace.

But his solitude was interrupted by the appearance of Moses who demanded that Pharaoh allow the Israelites to leave Egypt or else the Lord would send *arob*,[48] "swarms of insects" (including wasps, hornets, and other flying pests) that would fill their houses and afflict everyone from Pharaoh in his palace to the poorest peasant in his ramshackle hut.

This time, however, the Lord was going to separate (Heb., "sever") His people from the Egyptians, and they would be exempt from the pain and suffering to be borne by the Egyptians (Exodus 8:22-23).

The next day great swarms of insects appeared. They covered the land and invaded the houses of the Egyptians. So severe was the discomfort inflicted on the Egyptians that Pharaoh sent for Moses and Aaron, and said to them "Go, sacrifice to your God [but only] within the land" (Exodus 8:25). Moses refused this compromise, and explained that their sacrifices involved cattle and sheep, and inasmuch as the Egyptians considered these animals sacred, those who worshiped them would rise up and kill the Israelites.

---

48. *Arob* usually refers to flies whose bite is painful and develops irritating lesions, but *arob* is also used of men in Exodus 12:38.

Pharaoh saw the wisdom of Moses' argument and proposed a further compromise. "I will let you go to offer sacrifices to *Yahweh* your God in the desert, but you must not go very far. Now pray for me" (Exodus 8:28). To this Moses agreed, but he warned Pharaoh not to "deal deceitfully" again with God or His people (cf. Exodus 8:8, 15).

Moses prayed to the Lord for the flying insects to be removed, and they were taken away. Not one remained. However, as soon as Pharaoh found that the emissaries of God's judgment had been removed, he hardened his heart and would not let Israel go.[49]

The Fifth Judgment: Disease on the Livestock (Exodus 9:1-7)

This plague was the immediate punishment for Pharaoh's obduracy. Until now God's judgments had brought physical discomfort, but now property also would affected.

Murrain is a very grievous sickness that attacks domestic animals. Egypt was primarily an agricultural country, yet the wealthy nobles prided themselves on the fine quality of their horses, mules, cows, sheep and goats, and even the different Pharaohs boasted of their vast flocks and herds (cf. Genesis 47:6).

---

49. Those who are prone to accuse God of being calloused and hardening Pharaoh's heart overlook Exodus 8:15, 19*b*, 32. See also Psalm 36:1-4.

Murrain in Egypt is often very violent. It usually appears in November/December when, with the receding of the water of the Nile, the cattle are turned out into the fields. There is a record of one particularly severe outbreak when nearly all the cattle died as a result of the plague.

In Egypt, all over the land, from the eastern frontier, where camels were bred for trade with Syria and Arabia, to the extreme west where Egypt merged with Libya, and for a thousand miles to the south where travelers encounter the First Cataract, there were evidences of the disease. To be compelled to listen to the moaning of the cattle must have been heart-wrenching, and to watch the horses, mules, sheep and goats, stagger about before sinking to the ground where they died, must have caused their owners to wonder if they would ever regain their wealth.

And with the advance of the plague large numbers of herdsmen became unemployed.

The basic lesson being forced upon Pharaoh was the fact that life and death were in the hands of Israel's God. The invisible boundary line between Egyptians and God's people in Goshen continued. And life among the Hebrews went on as before. Pharaoh could not believe that the Israelites were exempt from this plague and sent men to investigate. They returned to him and reported that among the Israelites all was well.

This judgment, like the others, revealed the powerlessness of Egypt's gods. Cows were sacred to Isis;[50] goats were worshiped at Mendes and sheep at Thebes. Hathor,[51] the sacred cow, was venerated as the goddess of love; the Apis-Bull of Memphis and the Mnevis-Bull[52] of Heliopolis were the objects of reverential awe. The fact that these gods were discredited by this judgment must have begun to seriously weaken the Egyptians' belief system.

The Sixth Judgment: Boils on Man And Beast (Exodus 9:8-12)

The sixth judgment came without prior warning. The Lord commanded Moses and Aaron to take ashes from the furnace. Then, when they confronted Pharaoh, Moses was to throw the ash toward heaven where it became small dust that blew all over Egypt. This dust then caused boils to break out with sores on men and animals. Moses did so, and the result was so devastating that the magicians could not stand before Moses.

This judgment was provoked by the pride and obstinacy of Pharaoh, who had taken no notice of the preceding problems inflicted on Egypt's people and livestock.

The Seventh Judgment: Hail (Exodus 9:13-35)

Whereas no specific announcement had preceded the previous judgment, the Lord now told Moses to give Pharaoh a solemn warning.

---

50. Watterson, *The Gods of Ancient Egypt*, 60-62, 78-81, 87-89.
51. Ibid., 124-33.
52. Ibid., 68, 79, 165-66.

"Thus says *Yahweh*, the God of the Hebrews, 'Let My people go, that they may serve Me. For this time I will send all My plagues on you and your servants and your people, so that you may know that there is no one like Me in all the earth. For if by now I had put forth My hand and struck you and your people with pestilence, you would then have been cut off from the earth. But, indeed, for this reason I have allowed you to remain, in order to show you My power and in order to proclaim My name through all the earth. Still you exalt yourself against My people by not letting them go. Look, about this time tomorrow, I will send a very severe hail storm upon the land, such as has not been seen in Egypt from the day it was founded until now" (Exodus (:13-18)

This warning was accompanied by a recommendation that all servants and livestock presently in the field be brought to safety so that they would not be killed by the hail. Only the land of Goshen would be spared. The Lord then told Moses to stretch out his staff toward heaven, and the sky grew black, the wind increased in its force, thick clouds appeared to buffet each other as they moved along, the thunder crackled, and flashes of lightening terrified man and beast. As promised, the Lord sent hail upon the land. The whole canopy of heaven was lit up while huge hail stones fell to the ground. All plant life was decimated, and the animals that had not been safely housed in a covered enclosure were killed (cf. Psalms 18:13; 78:47-48; and105:32).[53] And any humans who ignored the warning died.

Once again those in Goshen were spared.

The god Serpes and the goddesses Nut and Hathor lived in the trees, and they were shown to be completely power-less to prevent the devastation that resulted from the hail. Nut[54] was also to blame, for she was the sky goddess; and Reshpu and Ketesh were likewise shown to be impotent, for they were supposed to control the elements.

Pharaoh sent for Moses and Aaron. When they appeared before him, he said: "I have sinned ... Make sup-plication to *Yahweh*, for there has been enough of God's thunder and hail. I will let you go, and you shall stay no longer."

Moses prayed to the Lord and the thunder and hail ceased, and for a brief time the spirit of the king was hum-bled. His servants probably reported to him that the barley and flax crops had been completely destroyed, but when he realized that the wheat and spelt crops had not been harmed, he stubbornly refused to let the Israelites go.

The Eighth Judgment: Locusts (Exodus 10:1-20)

Once again the Lord spoke to Moses and Aaron and told them to go to Pharaoh and announce the coming of swarms of locusts. The wheat and the spelt that had not been destroyed by the hail (because the seeds that had been sown had not sprouted out of the ground). These crops would now be eaten up by these ravenous insects that would

---

53. See also Josephus, *Antiquities of the Jews*, II:14:4.

54. Watterson, *The Gods of Ancient Egypt*, 48-52.

cover the land like an invading army (cf. Joel 1:4, 6-7; 2:2-9; Nahum 3:17).[55]

It is evident from Exodus 10:3-6 that God's patience was wearing thin. So far Pharaoh had ignored God's gracious warnings of coming judgments, but now his courtiers came to him and pleaded with him to let the Israelites go, because Egypt was being destroyed by *Yahweh*'s judgments. But Pharaoh refused. Perhaps he prided himself on the fact that the god Senehem (pictured in ancient Egyptian drawings as a locust) would protect them. At the entreaty of his servants he decided to offer Moses and Aaron a *compromise*: Only the male Israelites could go.

This compromise was unacceptable, and Moses explained that everyone would go--the young as well as the old, their sons as well as their daughters, their flocks as well as their herds.

With this, Pharaoh flew into a rage and had God's messengers removed from his presence (Exodus 10:10-11). He thought that by offering Moses and Aaron a concession he could outwardly appear to be a benign and indulgent ruler while at the same time retaining his power over the Israelites. Moses showed him that compromise is never anything

---

55. See H. B. Tristram, *The Natural History of the Bible* (1898), 306-18; J. D. Whiting, *National Geographic Magazine* 28 (December 1915), 512-50; T. Chapelle and D. Chapelle, *National Geographic Magazine* 103 (April 1953), 545-62; and R. A. M. Conley, *National Geographic Magazine* 136 (August 1969), 202-27.

but an ignoble truce between the will of God on the one hand and the self-will of man on the other.

The Lord then told Moses to stretch out his staff over the land of Egypt. He did so, and the Lord sent a strong east wind that blew all day and all night. By the next morning the ground was covered with locusts that ate up everything the hail had left. They ate the wheat and rye crops, the grasses that had been flattened by the hail, the clover and lentils, the onions and leeks, gourds and cucumbers, the date-bearing palms, figs and pomegranates, the fruit that had begun to form, and even the bark of the trees. The land that had previously looked like the garden of Eden was left a desolate wilderness.

In desperation Pharaoh sent for Moses and Aaron, and respectfully asked for the locusts to be removed. Moses prayed to the Lord, and He sent a strong west wind that blew all the locusts into the Red Sea. Once the locusts had been removed Pharaoh felt both relief and anger. He was relieved that the locusts were gone, but angry over what had happened to his land. In this rebellious frame of mind the Lord hardened his heart, and he would not let the Israelites go.

The Ninth Judgment: Darkness (Exodus 10:21-29)

With the hardening of Pharaoh's heart the Lord sent the ninth plague on the land of Egypt. Like the third and sixth judgments, this one came unannounced. The Lord told Moses to "Stretch out your hand toward the sky so that darkness will spread over Egypt--darkness that can be felt." No explanation is given us as to how this phenomenon occurred.

Moses obeyed and stretched out his hand toward the sky, and total darkness covered all Egypt for three days. No one could see anyone else or leave his/her place for three days. Yet all the Israelites had light where they lived.

This judgment was against Ra, the sun god.[56] The miraculous veil of darkness lasted for seventy-two hours. Each person stood or sat exactly where he was when the sun's rays were darkened, and no one was able to move. When the darkness finally disappeared and the sun reappeared it was found that Ra had not fallen from his place in the heavens, nor had he been extinguished by some primeval darkness.

To the Egyptians, however, what had happened had been sufficient to shake their belief in Ra's supremacy and omnipotent power. And Pharaoh, who was supposed to be the son of Ra, was likewise shaken, for he had been shown to be both inept and impotent. And now he was to prove that he was also indecisive. He summoned Moses and said, "Go, worship *Yahweh*. Even your women and children may go with you; only leave your flocks and herds behind." *This was his last attempt at compromise.* Pharaoh knew that if the Israelites left their livestock behind they would have to return.

---

56. Watterson, *The Gods of Ancient Egypt*, 33, 41, 44–45, 49.

"But Moses said, 'You must allow us to have sacrifices and burnt offerings to present to *Yahweh* our God. Our livestock too must go with us; not a hoof is to be left behind. We have to use some of them in worshiping *Yahweh* our God, and until we get there we will not know what we are to use to worship *Yahweh*'" (Exodus 10:25-26).

Pharaoh responded in anger and told Moses to get out of his sight, and to make sure he did not appear before him again. Then he added, "The day you see my face you will die."

Moses was conscious that he stood in the place of God, and so Pharaoh's rejection of him was in reality a rejection of God Himself,[57] and he responded, "You are right; I shall never see your face again."

The Tenth Judgment: Death of the Firstborn (Exodus 11:1–12:36)

As Moses left Pharaoh's presence he uttered one last prediction, "Thus says *Yahweh*, 'About midnight I will go out into the midst of Egypt; and all the firstborn in the land of Egypt shall die, from the firstborn of Pharaoh who sits on his throne, even to the firstborn of the female servant who is behind the millstone, and all the firstborn of the animals. Then there shall be a great cry throughout all the land of Egypt, such as was not like it before, nor shall be like it again. But against none of the children of Israel shall a dog

---

57. The story is interrupted by a brief parenthesis (Exodus 11:1-3), then it continues with verses 4-8.

move its tongue,[58] against man or beast, that *Yahweh* does make a difference between the Egyptians and the Israelites.' All these your servants will come down to me and bow down to me, saying, 'Go out, you and all the people who follow you!' After that I will go out." Then he went out from Pharaoh in great anger (Exodus 11:4-8).

And so it happened. When the Israelites were in their homes celebrating the Passover, the Lord passed through the land of Egypt and the angel of death struck down all the firstborn, both man and beast, and in this way executed judgment against all the gods of Egypt. In Goshen, however, the Israelites had placed the blood of the paschal lamb over the lintel and on the doorposts of their homes, and when the blood was seen no harm came to those inside the house. Their faith in the sacrifice of the lamb saved them.

Christians have seized on the typology of the blood applied to the doorposts and lintel of the homes of the Israelites as an illustration of the blood of Christ shed on their behalf. Around the year 1605 an unknown priest wrote of the victory believer's have in Christ.

> The strife is o'er–the battle done,
>   the victory of life is won;
> The song of triumph has begun:
>   Alleluia!

---

58. A proverbial expression meaning that the Israelites would be undisturbed.

Something to Think About

- It is easy for us to focus on God's punishment of the Egyptians, but let us also note how often the Lord dealt graciously with Pharaoh by warning him of what was coming. And let us take to heart how He also warns us when our conduct is not in keeping with His revealed will.

- Why did God allow the Israelites to endure with the Egyptians the first three judgments, but not judgments four through ten? Was it to show His sovereignty over all the people of the earth, or was it to demonstrate to Pharaoh that the Israelites were the special object of His care?

- For centuries Christians and non-Christians alike have felt that God was unjust in hardening Pharaoh's heart.[59] Have they confused His foreknowledge of what would take place with his judicial punishment of Pharaoh's wilfulness?

---

59. For an extensive consideration, see the discussion by the Swiss evangelical theologian, Louis Gaussen, in his book *From Egypt to Sinai* (London: Religious Tract Society, n.d.), 149-58.

CHAPTER SIX

LIBERTY AT LAST

Exodus 12:1-51 has been called the supreme chapter of the book of Exodus. In these verses are contained a record of the events that led up to the "going out" of the Israelites from Egypt. The information penned by Moses also described the last dread plague which provided the impetus for the festival that commemorated this great historic event.

The New Beginning (Exodus 12:1-2)

The deliverance of God's firstborn from servitude required something special to serve as a reminder to future generations of what the Lord had done. He, therefore, gave Moses and Aaron specific instructions: "This month shall be the beginning of months for you; it is to be the first month of the year to you." Then He stipulated how this distinctive feast was to be inaugurated.

The New Feast (Exodus 12:3-13)

The feast that Moses instituted became known as the "Passover." It's preparation required that on the 10th of the month the head of each Israelite family take a one-year old lamb without blemish, either from among the sheep or the goats, and keep it until the 14th day of the month. Then, toward sundown (i.e., sometime between 3:00 p.m. and 6:00 p.m. our time) it was to be killed. The head of the family was to catch some of the blood in a basin. This done, he was to take some hyssop and use it to sprinkle the blood on the doorposts and lintel of the door leading into the house in which the meal would be eaten.[60]

This was *done in obedience* to the word of the Lord, for He had said: "I will pass through the land of Egypt on that night, and will strike all the firstborn in the land of Egypt, both man and beast; and against all the gods of Egypt I will execute judgment: I am *Yahweh*."

Sprinkling the doorposts and lintel of the door with blood was also *an act of faith*, and it finds a parallel in the blood of the Lamb (Christ) that was shed so that all who trust Him for their eternal salvation have eternal life.[61]

The lamb that had been killed was to be roasted and eaten with unleavened bread and bitter herbs. It was to be wholly consumed. If, however, some of it remained until morning, it was to be burned up. Everyone who took part in the meal was to be dressed for a hasty departure. This necessitated that their long-flowing clothing be wrapped about their bodies, their sandals be strapped onto their feet, and their staff in their hand. These preparations signified that they were ready to start their journey toward the Promised Land.[62]

---

60. The Hebrew name for this month was Abib (but later on, its Babylonian name was Nisan, cf. Nehemiah 2:1; Esther 3:7). The days of Abib cover the later part of March and the first part of April. The middle of the month corresponds with our Easter which is generally held on the first Sunday after the first full moon following the vernal equinox.

Now let us imagine a typical home. The whole family is present: grandparents, parents, children, grandchildren. Of particular interest are the elderly. During their youth and early adulthood they had doubtless heard the story of how God had appeared to their forefather Abraham and promised him the land of Canaan as an inheritance. As they had grown older the harsh oppression of the Egyptians had caused the hope of freedom, that at one time had burned brightly in their hearts, to fade until it was barely a memory.

When Moses and Aaron had arrived they promised God's help in delivering them from slavery, and this caused the embers of their hope to glow. Now the day had arrived. As the grandfather and grandmother anticipated eating the Passover meal a faint sparkle once again lit up their eyes. Their wrinkled faces broke out in a smile as they clutched each other's hand, and their hearts beat a little faster as they contemplated the freedom that soon would be theirs.

---

61. Hyssop was a common type of grass that grew in tufts. Leaven, in Scripture, became a symbol of sin, and served to remind them of the need to separate themselves from the evils that had surrounded them in Egypt. Bitter herbs was to remind the Israelites of the rigors of their slavery.

It is significant that the Israelites were commanded not to break a single bone of the lamb (Exodus 12:46). When the Lord Jesus was crucified and a soldier came to break the legs of those crucified with Christ, and thus hasten their death, he pierced the side of the Lord Jesus. When he saw water and blood come from the wound he realized that He was dead already, and so did not break His legs (John 19:33-36).

Their son and daughter-in-law shared in the expectation of deliverance from slavery. They had strapped bundles on their backs containing the things they would need as they began their new life. The husband may have taken some of his farming equipment, and his wife would naturally have taken a few pots with the unleavened dough wrapped in a cloth and placed in a pan. And their grandchildren would have anxiously placed in a bundle a few of their favorite playthings.

According to the instructions given them by Moses, the Israelites were to eat the Passover lamb in a spirit of expectation. Their journey to their real homeland was soon to begin. And the same spirit of anticipation should be true of us today. We should live daily in hope of the Lord's soon return, for as the Apostle Paul said, we should do this knowing that our salvation is nearer to us now than when we believed (Romans 13:11).

The Passover reminds us of the justice and severity of God as He stands ready to punish unbelief and persistent sin (as He did the Egyptians for failing to turn to Him when they saw His signs and wonders against their gods), and of His desire to pardon all who turn to Him in faith and receive

---

62. The New Testament sheds light on the symbolism of the Passover. The Lord Jesus Christ is called "our Passover" (1 Corinthians 5:7) who sacrificed Himself that He might redeem us and cause us to pass from death to life (1 John 3:14; cf. Acts 26:18). He also became a fitting example of one who was gentle and meek and humble of heart, whose sufferings climaxed in His death on the cross of Calvary (cf. John 1:29, 36; see also Isaiah 53:7; and 1 Peter 1:19).

from Him the gift of deliverance from the wrath to come.[63] And the Apostle Paul admonished those of us who meet at the Lord's Table to clean out the old leaven so that we may be a new lump, for Christ our Passover has been sacrificed for us, and we are to celebrate our salvation not with the old leaven of malice and wickedness, but with the unleavened bread of sincerity and truth (cf. 1 Corinthians 5:7-9).

The Feast of Unleavened Bread (Exodus 12:14-28)

The feast of Unleavened Bread was intimately connected with the Passover.[64] Strangers or foreigners born in the land were not permitted to partake of the Passover meal unless they had come to faith in the Lord and demonstrated their belief by being circumcised.

The Death of Egypt's Firstborn (Exodus 12:29-43)

As we have already noted, at midnight, as the Israelites ate the Passover lamb in their homes, the Lord, accompa-

---

63. In the New Testament this involves a believer's salvation from eternal punishment (cf. John 3:15, 36; 5:24; 1 John 5:11-12).
64. *Massa* in the Old Testament was a figure used of what was to come, for in the New Testament the metaphorical use of leaven invariably had an evil connotation implying a corrupting influence (see 1 Corinthians 5:6ff., and Galatians 5:9). As always, George Bush, in his comments on *Genesis*, I:142, 145-46, has made many judicious observations on the biblical text.

nied by the "destroying angel," "struck down all the first-born in Egypt, from the firstborn of Pharaoh, who sat on the throne, to the firstborn of the prisoner, who was in the dungeon, and the firstborn of all the livestock as well" (Exodus 12:29)

When pondering these events Dr. George Bush asked the poignant question, "How shall we conceive of the complicated horrors of that fearful eve? The groans of the dying mingled with the shrieks of the living, broke upon the stillness of the night, and from the imperial palace to the poorest hovel, lamentation and mourning and woe were heard throughout the length and breadth of the land!"[65]

With the death of the heir-apparent in the palace, Pharaoh sent for Moses and Aaron and said, "Up! Leave my people, you and the Israelites! Go, worship *Yahweh* as you have requested. Take your flocks and herds, as you have said, and go." He dared not stand in the way of Moses' God any longer. His pride and trust in his own deity had been crushed, and he yielded unreservedly to all that Moses' had previously requested. Then, as a passing comment, he asked that Moses "bless him also" (Exodus 12:31-32).

The feeling of panic that Pharaoh felt was shared by every Egyptian family. They implored the Israelites to hurry and leave the country, for they believed that the Hebrew God might kill them too.

---

65. Dr. George Bush, *Exodus*, I: 148-49

The Departure From Egypt (Exodus 12:37-51)

The Israelites journeyed from Rameses to Succoth. There were about six hundred thousand men on foot, besides women and children. Many other people went up with them, as well as large droves of livestock. Their procession was a slow one, and it is doubtful if they covered more than ten or twelve miles a day. On reaching Succoth they camped for the night and the women baked cakes of unleavened bread with the dough they had brought with them. The dough they used was without yeast, and this became the basis of the Feast of Unleavened Bread.

If each of the 600,000 men on foot had a wife, which is likely, then the adults would have comprised 1,200,000. And if each couple had only two children, then those who left Egypt would have been in excess of two million people. Added to this number was a group that the Bible refers to as the "mixed multitude" (Exodus 12:37-38).

Moses also instructed Aaron regarding the future observance of the Passover that was to herald the beginning of each new year. It's importance is as follows:

"This is the ordinance of the Passover: no foreigner is to eat of it; but every man's slave purchased with money, after you have circumcised him, then he may eat of it. A sojourner or a hired servant shall not eat of it. It is to be eaten in a single house; you are not to bring forth any of the flesh outside of the house, nor are you to break any bone of it. All the congregation of Israel are to celebrate this. But if a stranger sojourns with you, and celebrates

the Passover to *Yahweh*, let all his males be circumcised,
and then let him come near to celebrate it; and he shall
be like a native of the land. But no uncircumcised person may eat of it. The same law shall apply to the native
as to the stranger who sojourns among you" (Exodus
12:43-44).

"O God, our help in ages past, our hope for years to
come,
    Be Thou our guide while life shall last, and our eter-
nal home."

For the Israelites, as well as for us, these words have a
special meaning.[66]

Something to Think About

When we consider the Passover in light of 1 Corinthians 5:7 and 1 Peter 1:18 we come to understand how
important are the times when we meet about the Lord's
Table. Consider, for example, ...

- As we partake of the bread and the wine we have
  time to reflect on our perfect redemption: past,
  present, and future.

---

66. Issac Watts, (1674-1748) and found in most hymnals.

- Our Communion service reminds us of God's perfect requirement (i.e., the blood of a spotless Lamb, namely, Christ). See John 3:16.

- When we consider John 6:54-57 the Lord's Table hints at *spiritual* strength for our journey by enabling us to draw inspiration and strength from Christ's life.

In light of these assurances we are absolutely safe and have complete absolute assurance of our salvation (see 1 John 5:11-12).

CHAPTER SEVEN

OPERATION: EXODUS

As the first blush of dawn began to shed its light on the desert sands stretching toward the eastern border of Egypt, the Israelite families began to stir. The air was fresh and, as here and there the men arose from lying on the ground (where they and their families had spent the night), they inhaled deeply the air of freedom and stretched out their arms as if to embrace the whole world.

They were free ... and freedom felt good!

The women fanned into a low flame the embers of the previous day's fire, and then began to prepare unleavened bread for the family to eat.[67] It wasn't long before Moses gave instructions for the camp of Israel to move out in an orderly way (Exodus 12:51). His directions, of course, were communicated to the leader of each tribe, and they in turn communicated the message to the head of each family. Since there were no electronic systems of communication in those days, and all instructions had to be passed on by word-of-mouth.

---

67. If all leaven had been removed from Israelite homes before they left Egypt, where did they obtain leaven once it was permissible to again to used in cooking? They probably used certain juices, that when added as a fermenting agent, leaven new dough.

This done, they began their march away from the land in which they had been in bondage. But freedom carries with it responsibility. Charles Kingsley opined:

There will be no true freedom without virtue,
No true science without religion,
No true industry without the fear of God
and love to your fellow-citizens.[68]

To lack such moral values is to pave the way for disunity, oppression and eventual anarchy.

As the Israelites marched toward the desert their hearts rejoiced because they were now full of hope. The Lord had done great things for them, and they were glad.[69]

The Dedication of the Firstborn (Exodus 13:1-16)

There are some special emphases in these verses, and one is the importance of children. The Lord emphasized this when He commanded Moses to consecrate to Him every firstborn male.

"The first offspring of every womb among the Israelites belongs to Me, whether man or animal" (Exodus 13:2).

---

68. From a placard issued by Kingsley in 1848.
69. Three times in these verses reference is made to the "strength of the Lord's hand" and His deliverance of Israel "with a stretched out arm."

The setting apart of the firstborn was to be accompanied by the eating of unleavened bread which reminded the Israelites of their great deliverance, but also assured them of future blessing (Exodus 13:5).[70]

Moses also stressed the fact that in the future, when children in a household would question the reason for the Passover ritual, their father would remind them of their slavery in Egypt, and testify "I do this because of what *Yahweh* did for me when I came out of Egypt" (Exodus 13:8). And years later, when a different generation would ask the same question, "What does this mean?" a father would be able to say, "With a mighty hand *Yahweh* brought us out of Egypt, out of the land of slavery" (Exodus 13:14).[71]

It should be noted that false religions are invariably started *for* adults. The goal is frequently the enrichment of the founders. Only in true religion is there an emphasis on the right relationship of little children to the Lord of glory. And the one place where this instruction should take place is the home. The home is the "laboratory" of life, and it is the father's responsibility, with the help of his wife, to jealously safeguard his children's spiritual nurture.

---

70. Unger, in his *Commentary on the Old Testament*, 116, has this to say: "Basic to holiness, both positional and experiential, is redemption from bondage (the penalty and power of sin). Salvation is unto a holy life. This is the reason why Moses emphasized the importance of the Feast of Unleavened Bread (cf. 12:15-20), as a perpetual ordinance stressing holy separation of the redeemed."

71. See also Deuteronomy 29:10-11; and for more general instruction of children, Deuteronomy 6:6-7.

The fact that the deliverance of the Israelites from Egypt was accompanied by the eating of unleavened bread gave rise to the Feast of Unleavened Bread that was celebrated each year immediately following Passover (cf. Exodus 12:1-20). It was to be a memorial typifying holiness and separation of life. This is an important principle, particularly in our day when unwholesome ideas bombard our children via television programs, text messages, and an ever-increasing number of video games. And modern parents know that walking the proverbial tightrope between legalism and licence is not only difficult, but also requires constant vigilance as they try to keep pace with their children's changing needs.[72]

The Leading of the Lord (Exodus 13:17-22)

According to the *Macmillan Bible Atlas* most traffic leaving Egypt and traveling eastward would take one of three routes. The most direct route to Canaan was the *Via Maris* or "The Way of the Sea." The Egyptians called this road "The Way of [the god] Horus," and in verse 17 it is referred to as "The Way of the Land of the Philistines," but inasmuch as it followed the coastline the name *Via Maris* or the "Way of the Sea" was most appropriate.

God did not permit His people to travel along this road, even though it was the shortest and most convenient, because Egyptian fortresses had been built at intervals along

---

72. Some helpful hints may be obtained from the book by Barber and Strauss, *My Son, Jonah* (Eugene, OR: Wipf & Stock, 2010), 231pp.

it and He did not want His people to encounter strong resistance that might make them discouraged. He had also promised Moses that the people would worship Him at "the Mountain of God" in the southern part of the Sinai Peninsula (Exodus 3:12).

A second way to Canaan was "the Way of Shur," south of the *Via Maris*, with an important water-source along the way.

The third route was down the Sinai Peninsula along what is known today as "the Pilgrim Way." It runs south along the Gulf of Suez before turning eastward to the Gulf of Aqaba and then north to its head at Ezion-geber. This was also known as "the Way of the Wilderness of the Red Sea," and it was this way that the Israelites took (Exodus 13:18).

With all of the decisions that had to be made, Moses did not forget the request made by Joseph more than three-and-a-half centuries earlier (cf. Genesis 50:25; Exodus 13:19; Hebrews 11:22). He took with him the coffin or sarcophagus containing Joseph's remains so that Joseph's last resting place would be in the Land of Promise.

It was after the Israelites had set out from Succoth en route for Etham that the Lord began to lead His people via a cloud by day and a pillar of fire by night, and "He did not take away the pillar of cloud by day, nor the pillar of fire by night, from before the people." Later, after the Tabernacle had been built, the evidence of God's presence resided over the Holy of Holies. The cloud indicated when they should break camp and move on, and when they should set up camp (Numbers 9:15-23).

While still on the border of Egypt, facing the wilderness, the Lord gave specific directions to the Israelites to make camp facing Pihahiroth, and position themselves between Migdol and the sea.[73] From a human point of view it seemed as if God had led them into a trap. But in His sovereign wisdom He planned to forever break the control the Egyptians had exercised over them, and give His people a lasting demonstration of His power (cf. Psalms 66:6; 106:9-11).

The Deliverance From Their Enemies (Exodus 14:1-31)

When Pharaoh learned that the Israelites were apparently wandering about aimlessly, an idea formed quickly in his mind. He determined that he and his army should pursue them, capture them, and again subject them to forced labor (Exodus 14:5-7). He, therefore, instructed his people (i.e., his servants and palace guard) and his elite corp (with their six hundred chariots) and his mounted cavalry to prepare for

---

73. The exact identity of the Hebrew *yam sup*, "Red Sea" or "Sea of Reeds" has been hotly disputed by modern Bible critics, and this has given rise to endless debate. Earthquakes in the area over the past three thousand years have brought about changes in the topography that make precise identification difficult. After much research the brilliant Oxford historian, George Rawlinson, wrote: "The traditional beliefs of both the Egyptians and the Israelites that the sea was the Red Sea is in fact of such vast weight that, against it, geographical speculations and ingenious explanations of names, sink into insignificance, and are, to say the least, quite insufficient to establish a theory which runs counter to the belief of Bible students for three millennia."

immediate, rapid deployment. The chariots were swift running, light vehicles that had become famous in Egypt's wars against their enemies.

When all was ready the Egyptians pursued the Israelites and overtook them camping by the sea before Baal Zephon.[74] When the Israelites saw the Egyptian army, they were terrified (Exodus 14:9-10). Some cried out to the Lord, but others, having so soon forgotten God's remarkable intervention in delivering them from slavery, vented their feelings on Moses:

> "Is it because there were no graves in Egypt that you have taken us away to die in the wilderness? Why have you dealt with us in this way, bringing us out of Egypt? Is this not the word that we spoke to you in Egypt, saying, 'Leave us alone that we may serve the Egyptians'? For it would have been better for us to serve the Egyptians than to die in the wilderness" (Exodus 14:11-12).

Moses, who was the meekest[75] man on the face of the earth (see Numbers 12:3), did not take offense, nor did he respond to the specifics contained in their accusation. Instead, he spoke directly to their feelings of fear, and told them to "Stand firm and see the deliverance *Yahweh* will bring you today. The Egyptians you see today you will

---

74. The towns or villages mentioned in Exodus 14:2 have not been identified, and it is possible that they have been covered over by the shifting desert sand.

75. Meekness is not weakness, but strength under control.

never see again. *Yahweh* will fight for you; you need only to
be still" (Exodus 14:13-14).

The Parting of the Red Sea (Exodus 14:1-22). As
Moses prayed to the Lord He told him to "lift up your staff,
and stretch out your hand over the sea and divide it, and the
children of Israel shall go on dry ground through the midst
of the sea.... Then Moses stretched out his hand over the sea;
and *Yahweh* caused the sea to go back by a strong east wind
all that night, and made the sea into dry land, and the waters
were divided." But this was not all. The cloud, which was
the visible evidence of the presence of the Lord in their
midst, moved from in front of the Israelites to the rear of the
camp. In this way their enemies were forced to halt their
pursuit because of the thick darkness, whereas the Israelites
had the light of God's presence and were able to go into the
midst of the sea on the dry ground (Exodus 14:16, 19-22; cf.
Deuteronomy 4:24; 9:3).

The Destruction of Pharaoh's Army (Exodus 14:23-31).
The next day when the Egyptians saw what had happened,
they attempted to use the same sea bed to pursue the Israelites. As they did so the Lord caused the wheels of their
chariots come off (Exodus 14:25 NIV) or come loose, so
that they had difficulty driving. This caused great conster-
nation to the Egyptian army, and they said in effect, "Let's
get out of here, away from the Israelites, for their God is
fighting for them against Egypt."

At this precise time the Lord told Moses to stretch out
his hand over the sea so that the waters may flow back over
the Egyptians and their chariots and horsemen; and Moses

did so. At daybreak the sea went back to its place, and the water that had been like a wall on the right and left of the Israelites, swept over Pharaoh's army, covering both chariots and horsemen. Not a single member survived.

The Israelites saw what had happened, and experienced a new reverential awe of the Lord (Exodus 14:31), and also had renewed respect for Moses. And Moses, who had studied music and poetry when a student in Egypt, composed a new song for God's people to sing, and Miriam led the women in singing and dancing to the Lord (Exodus 15:1-21).

Something to Think About

God has never promised to keep us from the trials and difficulties of life, but He has promised that He will give us the grace to persevere. The help and protection He gave the Israelites at the Red Sea is a case in point. What He did then reminds us of the words of Fanny Crosby:

All the way my Savior leads me; what have I to ask beside?
Can I doubt His tender mercy, who through life has been my Guide?
Heavenly peace, divinest comfort, here by faith in Him to dwell!
For I know that whate're befall me, Jesus doeth all things well.

All the way my Savior leads me, cheers each winding path I tread,
Gives me grace for ev'ry trial, feeds me with the living bread.
Though my weary steps may falter, and my soul athirst may be,
Gushing from the Rock before me, lo! A spring of joy I see.

All the way my Savior leads me; Oh the fulness of His love!
Perfect rest to me is promised in my Father's house above.
When my spirit, clothed immortal, wings its flight to realms of day,
This my song through endless ages, Jesus led me all the way.

CHAPTER EIGHT

ALONG THE PILGRIM WAY

PART ONE

Some years ago, when on a book-buying trip for a university with satellite campuses in different parts of the world, I included in my itinerary A visit to Brighton, England. My visit did not meet with the success I had hoped for, and before leaving the city I decided to visit a "Mom-and-Pop" used bookstore I had noticed as I entered the city. I asked the attendant where the "religious" books were, and was told, "Up the stairs; the room on the left."

I quickly perused the shelves but failed to find anything of significance. I then began scanning the titles of those books on the floor. Among the plethora of dust-covered volumes I saw one slender, drab-looking work. It did not carry its title on the spine, but the title page informed me that it had been written by Major-General D. J. Wilson-Haffenden. Within its 61 pages I learned of the difficulties the author had faced when he was responsible for keeping the British Army in Arabia supplied with food and water during World War II.

What followed in General Haffenden's book was data I had not found in any other work. He estimated that for Moses to provide for more than 2,000,000 people with a minimum of one pound of food per day he would require the equivalent of two full train loads of supplies. Of course, there were no trains in those days, only camel caravans; but even if the people ate their sheep and cows—which they were most unlikely to do—their small flocks and herds would be quickly exhausted, and then they would have nothing to eat.

Firewood for cooking would amount to 2,400 tons every day, and inasmuch as the Israelites were traveling through the desert, the task of meeting this need would be well-nigh insurmountable.

Water for drinking and cooking would be of the utmost importance. Each person would consume about a gallon of water per day, and more would be needed for washing or bathing, and watering the flocks and herds. It is estimated that a good well would give about 6,000 gallons per hour, so that if it was worked continuously (and did not run dry) the user might get 72,000 gallons from it in a single day. General Haffenden then calculated that at least twenty-nine such wells would be required at each halting place for drinking needs of the Israelites. And the needs of the animals would have to be added to this figure. When he added up all these needs, the task facing Moses could only be accomplished with God's help.[76]

With Exodus 15:22–17:7 we come to a section of the book that contains the dissatisfaction of the people. In

---

76. D. J. Wilson-Haffenden, *Operation Exodus* (London: Marshall, Morgan & Scott, 1957), 17-19. This is only a brief resume of the data supplied in this book. I knew that the university would not have a need for this brief monograph, and so I paid the 4/6 (four shillings and six pence)—keeping the book for my personal use.

15:22-27 we find the people grumbling because they had no water. We might have expected that after the miracle of the parting of the Red Sea the people would have been filled with trust in their leader and the God whom he represented (cf. Exodus 14:31), but this was not the case.

From a positive review of all that happened we learn that the Lord never brings hindrances into our lives that He does not intend to use for our spiritual growth.

The Bitter Waters (Exodus 15:22-27)

Travelers in the desert know that three days is the maximum time the human body can go without water. After three days in the blistering hot desert sun, the water the Israelites brought with them had been used up, and they had begun to suffer from acute dehydration. Their throats were parched, and they were suffering from such listlessness that some may have begun to suffer from hallucinations.

But how could the Israelites have been so negligent as not to bring enough water for drinking purposes? They did not have canteens, though they probably carried water in goat skins. But once they ran out of water their plight became desperate. Now, with their physical endurance stretched to the limit, they faced the unknown with ever-increasing fear.

It was then that some people in the forefront of the column saw some palm trees in the distance. These most assuredly marked an oasis. Word quickly passed to those behind them, while those in the van rushed forward, falling over one another in their haste to get to the water. And the slow, sedate gait of the sheep and cattle also quickened as they smelled the water. The first to reach the oasis fell face down in the water, but after a couple of mouthfuls they straightened up and turned in anger on Moses. The water was so bitter it was well-nigh undrinkable.

These waters that the Israelites called "Marah," were beautiful to look at, but they were then and still are laced with calcium and magnesium.

But why did the Lord allow the people to experience such acute disappointment? Is He a sadist who gets satisfaction from watching people suffer? No! There was a purpose behind the experience of the people at Marah, and it is best explained by the Bedouin saying, "One spoonful and you go for a week."

The Holy Spirit who inspired this record further amplifies what the Bedouin meant. The Israelites had used water from the Nile for drinking, bathing, and washing their clothes. As a result they carried in their bodies parasites that caused illnesses such as amoebic dysentery and bilharzia,[77] to mention only two. The Lord's intent was for the waters of Marah to purge their bodies of all harmful organisms..

77. In the mid-Twentieth Century my brother contracted bilharzia. He had been camping with some friends along the bank of a river. This dread disease is caused by a snail-borne parasite that lives in slow-moving irrigation ditches or the backwaters of some streams. The result is a lassitude that sometimes results in death. My brother was fortunate; he recovered.

But what, we may ask, was Moses' reaction when the people complained so bitterly about the waters of Marah?

Had he been like many of us he might have turned in anger on the complainers, excoriated them for acting like troglodytes, and justified himself by pointing to all he had done for them. Instead he faced with equanimity the kind of situation we all face at one time or another. He may have been baffled by their angry outburst, especially as he recalled his experience at the burning bush when the Lord had assured him that He would rescue His people from slavery and lead them to the land He had sworn to give to Abraham, Isaac and Jacob (Exodus 3:7-12). But now, with the people in such a rage, God's promise was a far cry from Moses' present experience. And what was even more disturbing, the miraculous events at the Red Sea had not produced in the Israelites any permanent respect for the Lord or "His servant Moses" (cf. Exodus 14:13-14).

Moses sets us an example of what we should do when we face similar opposition and the seeming demise of our dreams. He prayed to the Lord. In answer, the Lord showed him a tree and told him to throw it into the waters. Moses probably began by cutting off the branches and tossing them into the pool, and then he did tho oame with the dismembered tree trunk.

The Bible's critics continuously try to minimize God's power and involvement, and attribute the sweetening of the water to sap in the tree. Certainly God may have used the chemical properties of the tree to bring about a change in the water, but the Bible states that it was obedience to the Lord's command that resulted in the waters becoming drinkable. Dr. Charles C. Ryrie stated the matter succinctly: "The Lord, not the tree, made the water drinkable."

We may presume that once the waters of Marah had been sweetened, all the Israelites and their cattle drank their full. Their experience reminds us of a spiritual parallel to these events in the experience of the psalmist. He applied the experience of the Israelites to his spiritual thirst, and wrote, "As the deer pants for the water brooks, so my soul pants for You, O God. My soul thirsts for God, for the living God ..." (Psalm 42:1), and the Lord Jesus invited all who experience a similar spiritual thirst to come to Him and drink (John 7:37).

Spiritual thirst is the dominating factor in the life of all human beings, and it can only be met in and through a vital relationship with Jesus Christ that begins with the new birth and continues as it is nourished through meditation on God's Word (Psalm 1:3; John 3:36; 1 Peter 2:2).

Elim's Idyllic Setting (Exodus 15:27)

The Israelites, having left Marah behind them, came within a short time to Elim. No one is entirely sure where the biblical Elim was, though it probably was no more than three to seven miles south of Marah. It is believed that it was in what is now known as the Wadi Feiran, where there is one of the most beautiful oases to be found in the Saudi Arabian peninsula. In this wadi the Israelites found twelve springs of water and seventy date palms.

This was an ideal setting in which the Israelites could rest, and here they experienced physical (and we hope, spiritual) renewal. As the psalmist sang in Psalm 23:2-3, "He makes me to lie down in green pastures; He leads me beside the still waters. He restores my soul; He leads me in the paths of righteousness for His name's sake."

But what is the significance of *springs of water* and *date palms*?

The Bible describes three different ways in which the people of antiquity obtained water for their daily needs. The hot climate and the needs of large flocks and herds made a supply of water a necessity (cf. Judges 1:15). One of the first instances of drawing water for the needs of one's livestock is found in Genesis 29:9ff., and another example is Moses who defended the rights of Jethro's daughters (Exodus 2:16ff.). And, of course, there was the daily routine of women in the village who drew water from the village well for the needs of their families (cf. 1 Samuel 9:11 and John 4:6ff.).[78]

---

78. I have adapted much of this material from Unger's *New Bible Dictionary*, 1363. Among Eastern nations wells have often involved questions of property, sometimes giving rise to serious contention. Thus Abraham opened the well Beersheba, and its possession was attested with special formality (Genesis 21:30-31). To acquire wells that the Israelites had not dug themselves was one of the marks of God's favor (Deuteronomy 6:11). To possess a well was considered a mark of independence (Proverbs 5:15); and to abstain from the use of wells belonging to others was a sign of respect for another person's property (Numbers 20:17,19; 21:22).

Water also came from cisterns and pits that had been dug for the purpose of capturing rainwater (cf. Proverbs 5:15; Ecclesiastes 12:6). Rain or spring water was cleverly directed to the cistern or pit that had been dug out of the rock. This was done so that water could be collected for use in the dry season. The mouth of the cistern was covered to limit evaporation. Cisterns that had no water in them, as well as those with mud at the bottom, were sometimes used as prisons (cf. Genesis 37:22; Jeremiah 38:6).

By far the most sought-after source of water, however, was from a spring. Running water was regarded as purer and tastier than well water. Neither cisterns nor wells give a sure supply of water, and only in water from a spring, that flows freely of its own accord, is there any certainty of a continuous supply. It was by means of twelve springs–one for each tribe–that the Lord met the needs of His people at Elim.

But what of the palm trees? In Hebrew they are referred to as *tamar*. The name most likely comes from its tall, straight, and slender stem.

Palm trees have been called the "princes of the vegetable kingdom." They have a cylindrical stem that is unbroken by branches. They are stately trees, rising high into the air unfurling a canopy of enormous leaves in the shadow of which are suspended great clusters of fruit. No tree growing in the desert could look more majestic or more bountiful.

The date-palm reaches a height of 30 or 40 feet (though some are twice as tall). It seldom bears fruit till six, eight, or even ten years after it has been planted; but it can continue to be productive for one hundred years (Psalm 92:14). If we were to limit its productive years to sixty or seventy years, and assign to it an average crop of 100 lbs. a year, each fruit-bearing tree would have yielded two or three tons of dates.

The palm grows slowly but steadily and is not influenced by those alternations of the seasons which affect other trees. It does not rejoice overmuch in winter's copious rain, nor does it droop under the drought and burning sun of summer. It stands, looking calmly down upon the world below, and patiently yields its large clusters of golden fruit from generation to generation.[79] Its stately elegance suggested to Solomon a valid comparison to a young, beautiful woman (Song of Solomon 7:7), and the psalmist saw in the palm tree a figure of the righteous enjoying their deserved prosperity (Psalm 92:12).

At Elim the Israelites, however, were glad to enjoy its fruit.

Something to Think About

I have profited greatly from the writings of Louis Gaussen, the Swiss evangelical theologian of a past generation. In one of his books he wrote: "There are two branches of wisdom most essential to our happiness and welfare, though they are treated by many with utter neglect. The first is a

---

79. See William M. Thomson, *The Land and the Book*, 3 vols. (New York: Harper & Brothers, 1886), I:65ff.

knowledge of ourselves (cf. Romans 7:18-20), and the second is a knowledge of God (John 17:3)."

Dr. Gaussen then quotes from 2 Thessalonians 1:7-10, and points out that there is coming a day when the "Lord Jesus shall be revealed from heaven with His mighty angels, in flaming fire taking vengeance of them that *know not* God, and do not obey the gospel of our Lord Jesus Christ." He continues, "The whole Bible is intended to give us this two-fold knowledge. We find it in its histories; some of them show us what man is, and others show us what God is." And, we might add, we find these two truths in the passage before us.

All too often we are like the Israelites. We are happy when events (like the overthrow of Pharaoh and his army) go our way, but the moment we are inconvenienced or suffer hardship we give way to feelings of anger and bitter criticism. All of this should teach us what we are like. But when we come to Exodus 15:27 we learn what God is like.

CHAPTER NINE

ALONG THE PILGRIM WAY

PART TWO

In our previous chapter we considered the conduct of the Israelites when they were faced with severe thirst. The needs of their families banished all other considerations from their minds, and in their present predicament we can imagine them trying to squeeze the last drop of water from their goatskin water bottles. Their dilemma was aggravated by the cries of their children as they pleaded with their mothers to give them something to drink; and their mothers naturally looked to their husbands to supply the needs of the family. Such deprivation leads to frustration, and we are not surprised that they turned in anger on Moses.

The conduct of the Israelites shows us the natural character in all of us. We all are prone to give way to ingratitude, vengeful thoughts, and even unbelief when faced with physical suffering.

This is in contrast to God's goodness, forbearance, gentleness, and longsuffering. As a loving Father He does not deal with us according to our sins, but is slow to anger, merciful, abundant in grace, and desires to reproduce in us qualities of truthfulness, uprightness of character, honesty, and righteousness, that are the marks of a godly character.

The Israelites were in God's "school." They had left Egypt one month earlier. Now, however, their new lesson was designed to teach them about patience, perseverance, and trust. This time the need that precipitated the crisis was hunger.

As we read Exodus 16 we note how their deliverance from Egypt had been wholly forgotten; the sting of the taskmaster's whip on their backs had faded into the gloomy recesses of their minds, and all they could think of was that in Egypt they had what to them seemed like a good diet of meat, bread, fish and vegetables.

Throughout this chapter we are reminded of the ingratitude of the Israelites. They grumbled against Moses, and their complaint showed that their Godward relationship had about as much depth as a birdbath. In spite of their incalcitrant spirit, the Lord continued to deal with them as His children.

The Journey (Exodus 16:1-3)

The Israelites had been journeying through the desert for a whole month when they came to the Wilderness of Sin. This probably was the wide and desolate plain of Markha, beyond Elim,[80] where the barrenness of the country presented a definite challenge to their food supply.

---

80. Some of the difficulties in identifying specific places have been discussed by Edward Robinson in his valuable *Biblical Researches in Palestine and Adjacent Regions*, 3 vols. (London: Murray, 1856), I:68-70.

But some will say, What of their numerous flocks and herds? First, we have no means of knowing how *numerous* were their sheep and goats and cattle, and how many animals would they have had to butcher in order to feed more than two million people? And how long would the meat derived from these animals have lasted? Second, pastoral people do not live upon the flesh of their animals, but upon the produce derived from them. They do slaughter a calf or a lamb when hospitality requires it, and they also offer a lamb or a bull on the altar for specific religious reasons.

Of importance to us, however, is Moses' response to the grumbling of the people. He knew before he went to Egypt to lead the Israelites out of bondage how humanly impossible would be such a task, and yet he did exactly what the Lord told him. His faith enabled him to believe that God could and would provide for His immense host. He had spent forty years caring for his father-in-law's sheep, and he knew better than anyone else the absence of resources for a flock of sheep, let alone a vast company of people.

Added to this burden that Moses bore, there was the morale of each husband and father. As they reflected on what they needed they were reminded of the abundance they had had in Egypt. Why shouldn't they go back to Egypt? Pharaoh's elite corp had been completely destroyed, and Pharaoh, they believed, had been so weakened that he could no longer oppress them. Why not return to Egypt? In Goshen, with its two crops a year, there would be an ample supply of food.

Their situation was a desperate one, and we are not surprised that they turned in resentment on Moses and Aaron, and said, "In Egypt we sat around pots of meat and ate all the food we wanted, but you have brought us out into this desert to starve this entire assembly to death" (Exodus 16:3).

It is part of human nature for us to quickly forget past problems and exaggerate past advantages, and to see the present through a single myopic lense. When this happens we little appreciate God's training methods. The writer of Hebrews asked, "have you forgotten that word of encouragement that God addresses you as sons:

'My son, do not make light of the Lord's discipline,
and do not lose heart when he rebukes you,
because the Lord disciplines those he loves,
and he punishes everyone he accepts as a son.'

"When you endure hardship as discipline, God is treating you as a son. For what son is not disciplined by his father? If you are not disciplined, then you are an illegitimate child and not a true son. We have all had human fathers who disciplined us, and we respected them for it. How much more should we submit to the Father of our spirits and live! Our fathers disciplined us for a little while as they thought best; *but God disciplines us for our good, that we may share in his holiness*. No discipline seems pleasant at the time, but painful. Later on, however, it produces a harvest of righteousness and peace for those who have been trained by it."[81]

God's Promise (Exodus 16:4-12)

There is an important lesson for all of us in the way in which the Lord dealt with His recalcitrant people. In response to their cynicism expressed in Psalm 78 when they asked scornfully, "Can God furnish a table in the wilderness?" there is His statement to Moses:

"Behold, I will rain bread from heaven for you. And the people shall go out and gather a certain quota every day, that I may test them, whether they will walk in My law or not. And it shall be on the sixth day that they shall prepare what they bring in, and it shall be twice as much as they gather daily." Then Moses and Aaron said to all the children of Israel, "At evening you shall know that *Yahweh* has brought you out of the land of Egypt. And in the morning you shall see *Yahweh's* glory; for He hears your complaints against Him. But what are we, that you complain against us?" Also Moses said, "This shall be seen when *Yahweh* gives you meat to eat in the evening, and in the morning bread to the full; for *Yahweh* hears your complaints which you make against Him. And what are we? Your complaints are not against us, but against the Lord."

God's promise of a miraculous supply of meat and bread was communicated to the people by Aaron. As they looked toward the wilderness. There they saw the glory of the Lord appear in the cloud. They had grown accustomed

---

81. A paraphrase of Hebrews 12:5-11. Emphasis added.

to the cloud ever since it protected them from Pharaoh's army.[82] Now, however, the cloud that they saw shone with a very intense light as the glory of the Lord shone through the cloud and filled the people with awe.

God then spoke to Moses and said, "I have heard the complaints of the children of Israel. Speak to them, saying, 'At twilight you shall eat meat, and in the morning you shall be filled with bread. And you shall know that I am *Yahweh* your God.'"

God's Provision (Exodus 16:13-36)

The Lord graciously undertook to meet the needs of the vast number of people who had left their homes in Egypt and followed His servant into the wilderness. An enormous flock of quail, tired after their long flight, either flew low over or came to rest in the camp. All the Israelites had to do was capture and prepare them for their evening meal.

But they were caught in such vast numbers that some method of preserving them became essential. How was this done? Dr. John Kitto, a renowned authority on Near and Middle Eastern customs and culture, answers the question. The Israelites knew that "the Egyptians lived much upon wild fowl. These birds were caught in large numbers, and needed to be preserved for future use. This was done by drying them in the sun, and perhaps slightly salting them." He then went on to point out that in Egyptian monuments

---

82. As the old adage goes, "Familiarity breeds contempt."

there are actual representations of birds, slit like fish, and laid out to dry.[83]

And this is probably what the Israelites did.

But what of God's provision of bread? The next morning the dew lay around about the camp. When it evaporated, there lay upon the surface of the ground a covering of small round substances that resembled hoarfrost. As the Israelites looked at this phenomenon, they said to each other in Hebrew, "*Man-hu,*" "What is it?" Moses then explained, "This is the bread that the Lord has given you to eat."

The round seed-like things that the Israelites gathered up were like coriander, white, with the taste of wafers made with honey and fresh oil (Exodus 16:31; Numbers 11:8). This manna was supplied to the Israelites year round for forty years, and ceased only when the Israelites crossed the River Jordan into the Promised Land. It fell in large quantities, so that each person could gather as much as he could eat. An *omer* was considered an adequate daily amount for each person.[84]

Moses also told the people that if more was gathered than could be eaten, it would spoil overnight, develop a foul odor, and breed worms. However, on the sixth day a double portion should be gathered in preparation for the Sabbath

83. *Kitto's Daily Bible Illustrations*, 2 vols. (Grand Rapids: Kregel, 1981), I:406-07.
84. In later periods, an *omer* was about two quarts, though it is uncertain how much an *omer* was at this time.

day. The Sabbath had not been instituted as a holy day (Exodus 20:9-11), but the Lord was preparing His people in advance for the legislation that Moses would institute.

Of course, there were some who disregarded what Moses told them, and they found out how costly disobedience is when they had to go hungry on the seventh day (cf. Deuteronomy 8:2-3).

As we allow ourselves to be transported back in time to those early mornings it fills us with reverence to see the multitudes of Israelites gathering every morning, from the desert sand, the bread which God in His goodness caused to rain down from heaven. And when we consider how the Lord Jesus used this Old Testament incident to speak of Himself, we begin to realize how important it is for each of us to daily spend time in the Word from which we draw nourishment for our daily needs (cf. John 6:35, 48).

Something to Think About

As Christians we need to take seriously the teaching of John 6, and in particular verse 35, where the Lord Jesus said of Himself, "I am the bread of life. He who comes to Me will never go hungry, and he who believes in Me will never be thirsty." The manna that kept the Israelites alive in the desert was a wonderful example of the way in which each person's needs is met by God's unfailing provision (John 6:32).

In grace the Lord appeared in His glory to the Israelites as they looked out over the barren desert waste of the Wilderness of Sin. What they saw impressed upon them the hopelessness of their situation. But God did not forsake them, even though they had complained about the way in which His servant Moses was leading them. And sorely tried believers through the centuries have found Him to be a very present help in time of trouble.

When some devout Christians in France were fleeing persecution, they sang about the close relationship they had with the Lord Jesus.

I have a Friend so precious,
So very dear to me!
He loves me with such tender love,
He loves so faithfully,
I could not live apart from Him,
I love to feel Him nigh;
And so we dwell together,
My Lord and I.

Sometimes I'm faint and weary;
He knows that I am weak,
And as He bids me lean on Him,
His help I gladly seek;
He leads me in the paths of light,
Beneath the sunny sky;
And so we walk, together,
My Lord and I.

He knows how much I love Him.
He knows I love Him well;
But with what love He loves me,
My tongue can never tell;
It is an everlasting love,
An ever rich supply;
And so we love each other,
My Lord and I.

Their words were later translated out of French into English.

CHAPTER TEN

ALONG THE PILGRIM WAY

PART THREE

The Bible is an exciting book. Each chapter contains light for our pilgrimage, nourishment for our souls, and a challenge to respond to what it reveals. William Cowper, the Christian poet and jurist said, "A glory guilds the sacred page, majestic like the sun; it gives its light to every age, it gives, but borrows none."[85]   And Exodus 17 is no exception.

As the chapter opens we are confronted with certain questions: Why did the Israelites journey "by stages" from the Wilderness of Sin to the plain of Rephidim?   Why wasn't there any water for the Israelites at Rephidim? After God's previous demonstrations of His ability to supply the needs of His people, why did the people grumble against Moses, and demand, "Is God among us or not?" (Exodus 17: 7*b*).   And why did Moses fear that the people would stone him?

The Journey to Rephidim (Exodus 17:1-7)

If we consult a topographical map of the Sinai peninsula[86] we note how easy it was for the Israelites, after leaving Egypt, to journey south following the coast of the gulf of

---

85. William Cowper (1731–1800).

Suez. After reaching the Wadi Feiran, however, they journeyed inland over very rocky terrain, and it was at this time
that they began to move forward "by stages." Our understanding is enlarged when we consult Numbers 33:11-14
and find that they made stops at Dophkah and Alush. The
valleys that extended eastward had a goodly supply of water
and grass for their sheep and cattle, but this disappeared as
they neared Rephidim.

The Lord, knowing full well that there was no water at
Rephidim, commanded[87] them to encamp there. Though
journeying at the express direction of the Lord, the people
were not immune from difficulties or distress. Their experience brings before us two important truths: (1) Being in
God's will does not exempt us from diverse trials; and (2)
The Lord has His reasons for bringing us into these quan-
dries. As we shall see, His plan was to supply their need by
creating for them an unforgetable "object lesson."

The Israelites, however, instead of remembering the
Lord's many gracious interventions in the past (cf. 1 Corinthians 10:11), grumbled[88] against Moses. In fact, they
became so angry that Moses began to fear for his life. An
evidence of their anger is to be found in their illogical claim

---

86. An excellent one is to be found in Carl G. Rasmussen's
    Atlas of the Bible, rev. ed. (Grand Rapids: Zondervan,
    2009), 69.
87. *At pi Yahweh*, "At the mouth of Yahweh." A similar state-
    ment is found in Numbers 9:18-19--made in connection
    with the movement of the cloud.
88. *Va-yareb*, from the root to strive, contend, litigate.

that Moses had deliberately brought them out into the desert to make them and their children and their livestock die of thirst.

Anger is fueled by feelings of frustration, humiliation, and rejection. These Israelite men, after searching diligently for water and being unable to find any, they become frustrated. They also felt humiliated when their children pleaded with them for water and their wives excoriated them for not making better preparations when water was plentiful. All of this led them to feel rejected as the leaders of their families. And in anger they turned on Moses.

But why were they so angry with Moses that he feared they might stone him? The answer to this question is probably linked with their demand, "Is *Yahweh* still among us or not?" They may have felt that either Moses had lost his way, or that some sin in the camp had caused the Lord to withdraw His support from them. Moses retained his accustomed calm demeanor and prayed to the Lord for His help. At a later time the psalmist found himself in a similar position and expressed the same kind of feelings Moses had when he prayed for God's timely intervention: "When I am afraid, I will put my trust in You. In God, whose word I praise, in God I have put my trust; I shall not be afraid. What can mere man do to me?" (Psalm 56:3-4).

The attitude of the Israelites also reminds us how ungrateful people can be, for the Lord had daily caused manna to rain down from heaven upon them (cf. Psalm 78:21-29, 32). Their conduct also reminds us that we, too, often take God's gifts for granted; and show little gratitude for all His goodness to us![89]

In answering Moses' prayer the Lord said to him, "Go on before the people, and take with you some of the elders of Israel. Also take in your hand your rod with which you struck the river Nile, and go. Behold, I will stand before you there on the rock in Horeb; and you shall strike the rock, and water will come out of it, that the people may drink." And Moses did so in the sight of the elders of Israel. So he called the name of the place Massah and Meribah, because of the contention of the children of Israel, and because they tempted *Yahweh*, saying, "Is *Yahweh* among us or not?" And the people completely slaked their thirst, and their sheep and cattle drank their fill (Exodus 17:5-7).

The fact that Moses called forth water from the rock serves as a "type"[90] for us. As we have noted before, the Lord Jesus is the fulfillment of this illustration, for He is the "living water" that fully quenches a believer's thirst. This

---

89. 1 Corinthians 10:1-11 spans the period of the exodus and shows how many and varied were the problems faced by Moses, and the numerous issues dealt with by the Lord.

90. A "type" is a divinely intended illustration of biblical truth that finds its fulfillment in later revelation. As the late Dr. Lewis Sperry Chafer stated, "Types and their antitype support the conclusion that God divinely framed human history to portray by illustration some of His future plans and purposes." See Chafer's *Systematic Theology*, abridged ed., 2 vols., eds. J. F. Walvoord, D. K. Campbell and R. B. Zuck (Grand Rapids: Zondervan, 1988), I:53.

was also the central part of Christ's teaching to the woman from Samaria (John 4:13-14; cf. 7:37-39).

Dr. Louis Gaussen commented on the names Moses gave the place where water gushed from the rock and completely slaked the thirst of the Israelites. He wrote:

> Moses called the name of the place Massah and Meribah, meaning temptation and chiding ... because they tempted the Lord, saying, "Is the Lord among us, or not?" How many moments are there in our lives, how many memories in our hearts, and connected with our homes, which we might call Massah and Meribah, because we have there tempted God! And we see from this verse that to tempt God is the same thing as to say, "Is the Lord among us, or not?" Thus the sin of tempting God is committed by the child of God who, having done wrong, having been disobedient and untruthful, says to himself, "Does God take notice of me, or does he not?" They equally tempt God, [when] like the scoffers, whose coming is foretold by the apostle Peter, they say, "Where is the promise of His coming? For since the fathers fell asleep, all things continue as they were from the beginning of creation" (2 Peter 3:4). Let us then, take heed to ourselves, and not tempt the Lord our God as the Israelites tempted him at Massah.[91]

Did the Israelites ask for God's forgiveness for doubting His kindness and for grumbling against His servant?

---

91. Gaussen, *From Egypt to Sinai*, 282-83.

No, they acted the same way we often do when we face life's disappointments.

Captain Scotty Smiley faced crushing disappointments. On April 6, 2005 he was blinded in both eyes when a suicide bomber blew himself up thirty meters in front of his vehicle. It seemed as if his promising career had suddenly come to an end; and worse still, he felt as if God had deserted him. For months he endured what others have described as the "dark night of the soul." With his wife's love and help, the support of his family and friends, and the prayers of many Christians in the United States and elsewhere, Scotty began to fight back. Today, though completely blind, he has achieved most of his dreams, teaches a course on leadership at West Point, and with Doug Crandall has written about his experience of God's faithfulness in spite of the trials he continues to face.[92]

The War With Amalek (Exodus 17:8-16)

The area where the Lord had miraculously supplied water from the rock and satisfied the thirst of the Israelites was then, and still is, a region marked by a very peculiar character. It is a vast limestone plateau with a very irregular surface, that projects like a huge wedge into the Red Sea. The general elevation of this plateau is about 2,000 feet above the sea. The ground is hard, and most of it is covered with sharp flint-like stones that have been sharpened and

92. Scotty Smiley with D. Crandall, *Hope Unseen* (New York: Howard, 2010), 235pp.

polished by the fine detritus sand that constantly blows over it.[93]

Animal life and vegetation are virtually nonexistent. It was certainly not the kind of place where the Israelites would want to settle, though it had been inhabited in remote antiquity by various wandering tribes. The discovery of copper and turquoise in the hills led to the establishment of Egyptian garrisons in the area, with the result that the land became denuded, so that by the time of Abraham (c. 2166–1991) the plateau was frequented only by traveling Bedouin.

While the Israelites were camped at Rephidim they encountered the Amalekites[94] The Amalekites were in all probability *the* most savage and inhumane tribe living in the Near East. They were well armed and disciplined for battle, having been accustomed to holding their own against other warlike neighbors. They looked upon the more than 2,000,000 Israelites living on the plateau as a gift from their god, and believed that they could easily defeat them in battle. After that they would plunder all they had. Without delay they took up their position in the most advantageous location, which was probably the Wadi Feiran, where they were protected by high hills on two sides.

The Wadi Feiran was easily defensible, whereas the Israelites were encamped in the open like flocks of defense-

---

93. Stanley, *Sinai and Palestine*, 18.
94. The Amalekites were most likely the descendants of Esau through his son Eliphaz.

less sheep. Moses realized the hostile intentions of the Amalekites and instructed Joshua to "choose out men for us and go out and fight against Amalek." And Joshua did so. Moses, with Aaron and Hur (Miriam's husband) beside him, stationed himself on the top of the mountain overlooking the plateau, and there, with his hands lifted up, he watched the battle below.

Moses' uplifted hands have caused many writers to conclude that he was drawing down the blessing of heaven upon the Israelite militia. In viewing the scene with the benefit of hindsight, Dr. Louis Gaussen wrote, "There were two things needful for Israel in the plains of Rephidim; it was necessary that Joshua should fight and that Moses should pray."[95]   Others, however, believe that Moses' upraised arms was a military signal for the Israelites to advance.

As the battle raged in the valley below him, Moses observed that first one side and then the other was successful in gaining the upper hand; and the success of Israel seemed to be connected with his upraised hands. As time passed his arms grew weary and he asked his brother Aaron and his brother-in-law Hur to help him. They placed a boulder in a strategic place and Moses sat on it. From this position he could watch the battle below, and Aaron and Hur helped by holding up his arms through the long, hot hours of the day.

---

95. Gaussen, *From Egypt* to *Sinai*, 292.

In the end Joshua and his hastily assembled force over-
whelmed the hostile aggressors, and were able to plunder
their enemy's goods. A Jewish historian of a later period
reflected upon the material and the moral effects of the victory:

> The material effects were twofold. In the first place
> there was a great accession of wealth to the Israelites,
> the Amalekites having taken to the field, as Orientals
> continually do, laden with gold and silver ornaments,
> and their camp being full of rich stuff, including vessels
> for the table both in bronze and precious metals, and of
> other valuable equipment. Second, the Israelites pos-
> sessed by their victory a large stock both of arms and
> armour, in which they had previously been very defi-
> cit....
> But the most important consequence of the victory,
> was the impression which it made upon the Amalekites
> themselves, and upon the other surrounding nations.
> Until the valour of Israel was tested, none could say
> whether a new nation had appeared [among them]...
> Amalek was completely defeated; after suffering great
> losses the Amalekite host had fled away in disorder
> from the field of battle. Israel had made itself respected,
> and the other minor tribes–Edomites, Moabites, Amor-
> ites, Philistines–were more respectful of Israel.[96]

After the victory *Yahweh* said to Moses, "Write this for
a memorial in a book and recount it in the hearing of Joshua,

---

96. Cf. Josephus, *Antiquities of the Jews*, III:2:57.

that *I will utterly blot out the remembrance of Amalek from under heaven.*" And the reason? When the Israelites came out of Egypt the Amalekites mercilessly attacked Israel's rear killing the sick and the stragglers, and plundering some of the goods that the Israelites had brought from Egypt (1 Samuel 15:2; cf. Deuteronomy 25:19).

Then Moses built an altar and called its name, *Jehovah-nissi*, "The Lord Is My Banner" (or more accurately, "The Lord is my 'rallying point'") in Israel's continuing war with Amalek.

Something to Think About

William Cowper dealt with some of the areas in which the Lord had been the rallying point of His people, when he wrote:

By whom was David taught,
  To aim the deadly blow,
When he Goliath fought,
  And laid the Gittite low?
Nor sword nor spear the stripling took,
But chose a pebble from the brook.

'Twas Israel's God and King,
  Who sent him to the fight;
Who gave him strength to sling,
  And skill to aim aright.
Ye feeble saints, your strength endures,
Because young David's GOD is yours.

Who ordered Gideon forth,
    To storm the invaders' camp,
With arms of little worth,
    A pitcher and a lamp?
The trumpets made his coming known,
And all the host was overthrown.

Oh! I have seen the day,
    When with a single word,
GOD helping me to say,
    My trust is in the LORD;
My soul's has quell'd a thousand foes,
Fearless of all that could oppose.

But unbelief, self-will,
    Self-righteousness and pride,
How often do they steal,
    My weapon from my side?
Yet David's LORD and Gideon's friend,
Will help his servant to the end.[97]

Having God as our "rallying point" is worthy of prolonged meditation. Here are three areas in which He can continuously be the center of our lives: In our marriages (Joshua 24:15), when teaching godly values in our children (Deuteronomy 6:2, 5, 7), and when we are enjoying the fellowship of our friends (Malachi 3:16-18). In these and other areas the Lord our God should constantly be the center around which all else revolves.`

---

97. *The Poetical Works of William Cowper*, ed. H. S. Milford (London: Oxford U. P., 1963), 435.

CHAPTER ELEVEN

ISRAEL AT THE BASE OF *JEBEL MUSA,*

THE MOUNT OF GOD

"In the third month [May-June] after the sons of Israel had gone out of the land of Egypt, on that very day they came into the wilderness of Sinai" (Exodus 19:1). They left the barren plateau of Rephidim, where the Lord had miraculously supplied water from the rock, and pitched their tents in the "wilderness of Sinai." Their journey took them onwards and upwards. They had good cause for rejoicing over their first victory, and with renewed confidence they advanced deeper and deeper into the mountain ranges, always following the cloud that went before them.

It is interesting for us to reminisce on the way the Lord led them. The Israelites did not know where they were going, but they trusted the Lord implicitly. Similarly, there are times in our lives when we do not know where the Lord is leading us, but we trust Him who is our Guide, and He never fails us.

As the Israelites went forward through winding valleys and under high cliffs, through rugged valleys and past gigantic forms on which the marks of creation seem forever to testify to the awesome power of God, they came to a broad passage that led to a level plain. Later travelers have measured this plain. It is about two-and-a-half miles long and half-a-mile wide; and to the north is the 7,500 foot mountain that has subsequently been identified as *Jebel Musa*, the "Mountain of Moses."

The semi-circular ring of mountains forms an amphitheater, and it became an ideal place for the giving of the Law. It was here, too, that Jethro, Moses' father-in-law came to visit his son-in-law.[98]

The Glad Reunion (Exodus 18:1-27).

Jethro had followed the activities of Moses in Egypt, and he had learned (possibly from traders leading caravans through Midian) of the destruction of Pharaoh's army. And now he was told that just a few days earlier, there had been the rout of the Amalekites. But most important of all, his interest had been aroused by all that God had done for His people.

Accompanying Jethro were Moses' wife, Zipporah, and *her* sons.[99] It must have been a happy occasion for Moses to be reunited with his family. Leaders often lead solitary lives, and the love and support of an understanding wife is a great blessing. We cannot read Exodus 18:7 without taking note of Moses' affectionate greeting of his father-in-law. While traditional, it was nonetheless sincere.

---

98. A. P. Stanley, *Lectures on the Jewish Church*, 3 vols. (London: Murray, 1875), I:127.
99. This is the last reference to Zipporah in the Bible. The fact that Moses' sons are identified with their mother is most unusual.

Moses and Jethro then retired into Moses' tent, and there Moses "told his father-in-law about everything *Yahweh* had done to Pharaoh and the Egyptians for Israel's sake and about all the hardships they had met along the way and how *Yahweh* had saved them. Jethro was delighted to hear about all the good things *Yahweh* had done for Israel in rescuing them from the hand of the Egyptians," and said, "Now I know that *Yahweh* is greater than all the gods."[100] Jethro then took burnt offerings and peace offerings, and offered them to *Yahweh* in gratitude for all He had done, and Moses and Aaron and Jethro, with the elders, sat down and enjoyed a meal together.

There are critics of the Bible who, building on the King James Version, claim that the events described in Exodus 18:12*b* could not have taken place at this time because the law respecting the priesthood and the sacrificial system had not been instituted. However, if we follow the New American Standard Bible all difficulties vanish. Furthermore, Jethro offered sacrifices in his capacity as a priest. And this solemn yet joyous celebration brought to a conclusion a most memorable day.

It is possible that the looting of the Amalekite camp caused some dissension among the Israelites. Perhaps those who were not selected to go to war felt left out when the spoils of war were divided among the militia. Whatever the

---

100. The repeated use of *Yahweh*, the name for the covenant-keeping God of Israel, in chapters 18:1–24:18 leads us to treat this section as a unit. The events described in these chapters also took place at the base of "the Mount of God."

reason, Moses felt it necessary to "hold court" and give judgment to each person as the Lord instructed him (Exodus 18:15).

It was a long and tiring procedure, and as Jethro watched he noticed that both Moses and the people were being worn out by the process. At the end of the day He counseled Moses to divide the people into groups and delegate authority to divisional leaders who would have the responsibility of judging on Moses' behalf.

These leaders were to meet specific criteria (Exodus 18:19-26): They were to be (1) Men who have demonstrated the capacity to lead (*anshe hayil*, men of strong character, active, efficient); (2) Men who have a strong reverential awe of God, who are conscientious, pious, and devout, who live each day with the conviction that the eye of the God of glory is upon them, and that they are accountable to Him; (3) Men of integrity whose word can be implicitly relied upon, and who cannot be seduced into betraying their trust; and (4) Men who hate covetousness and who manifest a positive abhorrence of the kind of corruption that is all too often linked with greed, selfishness, and all forms of bribery.

Moses listened to his father-in-law and chose men to fill these very necessary positions in Israel. Because the Lord moved to constitute Israel as a nation, the installation of these men as judges did not take place immediately (cf. Deuteronomy 1:15).

Jethro then proposed that he return to his people. Moses tried to dissuade him, but he declined. It would appear from Numbers 10:29 that his son Hobab remained with Moses at the insistence of Jethro, his father.

There are many important lessons to be gleaned from this chapter: the need for obedience; respect for one's elders; the place of gratitude; and the appropriate time for decisive action. Each person, however, can develop the traits that lead to usefulness.

The words made famous by Josiah Gilbert Holland (1819-1881) are worth committing to memory.

God give us men. A time like this demands
Strong minds, great hearts, true faith and ready hands!
Men whom the lust of office does not kill,
Men whom the spoils of office cannot buy,
Men who possess opinions and a will,
Men who love honor; men who will not lie.

Israel Constituted a Nation (Exodus 19:11-24:18)

The people gazed with reverential awe at Mount Sinai, and as they did so word spread via their leaders that it was somewhere in this mountain range that *Yahweh*, their covenant-keeping God, had met with Moses and sent him back to Egypt to liberate them from slavery. Now they were at the very place where the saga of their deliverance had begun.

The solemnity of the place and their arrival there was confirmed when they saw Moses ascending the mountain. There the Lord spoke directly to him, and said,

"This is what you shall say to the house of Jacob and tell to the people of Israel: 'You yourselves have seen what I did to the Egyptians, and how I bore you on eagles' wings,[101] and brought you to Myself. Now then, if you will indeed obey My voice and keep My covenant, then you shall be My own possession among all the peoples, for all the earth is Mine; and you shall be to Me a kingdom of priests and a holy nation.' These are the words that you shall speak to the sons of Israel" (Exodus 19:4-6).

Acting promptly, Moses descended the mountain and called the elders of the people to meet with him. He related to them all that the Lord had said to him, and they communicated the information to the people. The response was unanimous, "All that *Yahweh* has spoken we will do." The Israelites meant well, but they were ignorant of the weakness of the flesh. As Dr. Merrill F. Unger has pointed out, their history from that moment on is one long violation of that Law.[102]

Moses again ascended the mountain and related to the Lord all that the people had said. Because the Israelites

---

101. The Lord uses a beautiful figure of speech to describe His care of His people. The parent eagle, in teaching its nestlings to fly, sweeps gently past them as they perch on the ledge of the rock. When one, venturing to follow, begins to sink with drooping wing, the parent glides underneath it and bears it up again. (See Unger's *Commentary on the Old Testament*, 123.)

102. Unger, *Commentary on the Old Testament*, 123.

were familiar with the gods of Egypt who were visibly represented in the form of different animals or insects their curiosity would lead them to try to find out what God was like. *Yahweh* kew this, and that is why He stated that He would come to them in a thick cloud. He then instructed Moses to tell the people to consecrate themselves (i.e., set themselves apart) to Him by washing their bodies and their clothes (Exodus 19:10) in preparation for His coming on the third day.

To these stipulations, Moses added a third, *viz.*, abstaining from sexual intercourse. There is nothing wrong with sex between and a husband and his wife (cf. Hebrews 13:4). Such intimacy had been ordained by God from the time of creation. At this time, however, the Israelites were to abstain from all sex in order that their thoughts might be focused on the Lord and what He would say to them.

To further emphasize the fact that the Lord is altogether separate from the people the perimeter of the mountain was to be clearly identified, and any person or animal who breached the boundary was to die, either by stoning or by an arrow.

If the people had been in awe before, imagine their reaction when, on the morning of the third day "there were thunderings and lightnings, and a thick cloud on the mountain; and the sound of the ram's horn was so very loud that all the people who were in the camp trembled. Moses brought the people out of the camp to meet with God, and they stood at the foot of the mountain. Now Mount Sinai was completely covered in smoke, because *Yahweh* descended upon it in fire. Its smoke ascended like the smoke of a furnace, and the whole mountain quaked greatly. And *Yahweh* called Moses to the top of the mountain" (Exodus 19:16-20).

It is hard for us to imagine the impact all of this had on the people. They trembled with fear; but what they saw and heard prepared them for what *Yahweh* their God was about to say to them (Exodus 20:1ff.).

Then God spoke all these words, saying, "I am Yahweh your God, who brought you out of the land of Egypt, out of the house of slavery. You shall have no other gods before Me. You shall not make for yourself an idol, or any likeness of what is in heaven above or on the earth beneath or in the water under the earth. You shall not worship them or serve them; for I, *Yahweh* your God, am a jealous God, visiting the iniquity of the fathers on the children, on the third and the fourth generations of those who hate Me, but showing lovingkindness to thousands, to those who love Me and keep My commandments" (Exodus 20:1-6).

He then continued by ruling out profanity. What He said was literally, "You shall not lift up the name of Yahweh ... in vain" (cf. James 5:12). The intent of this command was to guard the deity of God.

After this God made the sanctity of the sabbath very specific. This commandment was never imposed on any nation or people except Israel, and it is the only law that does not find a place in the New Testament epistles. Its purpose was to illustrate the rest that the Lord has made for those who, by grace, obey His will and enter into the freedom of His children. Because the sabbath was a sign between the Lord and His people, profaning the day was a direct violation of the covenant (cf. Exodus 31:14-15; Numbers 15:32-35).

It seems strange to us that one of the commandments would focus on honoring one's parents. Many of us would consider it more appropriate if it were addressed to children today. Parents were then, and still are, God's representatives, and honoring them is honoring God.

God also stated emphatically, "You shall not murder" (cf. Matthew 5:21-22). This does not prevent a person from going to war, but only from taking a life deliberately and violently for selfish reasons.

Next, God safeguarded the sanctity of the home. Extramarital affairs between married people undermine the integrity of the family. The penalty for such conduct was very severe, viz., death (cf. Leviticus 20:10; Deuteronomy 22:22).

Safeguarding the integrity of the home is followed by safeguarding the rights of a person's property. Theft is a threat to society, and a society made up largely of thieves results in moral and social chaos.[103]

Honesty is the foundation of a civilized society. While the basic thrust of Exodus 20:16 has to do with testimony in courts of law (cf. Leviticus 19:18; Deuteronomy 19:16) the prohibition goes much further and covers all of a person's dealings with his/her neighbor (cf. Psalm 15:1ff.).

Finally, there is the warning against covetousness, which is a form of idolatry (Romans 7:7; 13:9). It stems from an inordinate desire for what one does not have, and has as its basis discontent with what the Lord has given. Covetousness leads to trust in "the uncertainty of riches," to love of the world, to forgetfulness of God, and is a form of idolatry (Colossians 3:5).

The ten commandments are followed by the social and ceremonial laws (Exodus 21:1–23:33).

The Israelites gladly accepted these laws, but they were soon to break them. In Exodus 32:1–34:35 the people gave in to their desire for a god whom they could see, and built the golden calf. Aaron proposed a type of syncretistic worship with which they were familiar, for it pervaded Egyptian religious practices.

The words "to play" in 32:6 are freighted with sexual overtones (cf. the usage of the same Hebrew word in Genesis 26:8), and when mingled with drinking resulted in intoxication and probable nakedness (cf. 1 Corinthians 10:8).

---

103. There are scores of books and journal articles on the Ten Commandments. Many rehash or refine the criticisms of past generations: see "The Code of Hammurabi," *New International Dictionary of Biblical Archaeology*, eds. E. M. Blaiklock and R. K. Harrison (Grand Rapids: Zondervan, 1982), 226-27.

Their actions brought down the wrath of God upon them, and Moses had to intercede for them. When the Lord's anger was turned away from His people Moses renewed the covenant they had made with the Lord.

God's people spent eleven months at the foot of Mount Sinai during which time they built the Tabernacle, and Moses wrote the book of Leviticus.

Something to Think About

As you reflect on Exodus 18–24, consider the evidence for God's power, sovereignty, presence, work, and awesome holiness; and then add to this the importance of knowing and doing His will.

At Sinai the Israelites were inducted into a special covenant with special laws (note Deuteronomy 4:8). As you reflect on the covenant He established, think specifically of its privilege (given to the "sons of Israel"), its uniqueness (Israel to be God's own possession among all the nations on the earth), and purpose (Israel to be a kingdom of priests and a holy nation).

In the Moral Law (Exodus 20:1-12), and the Social and Ceremonial Laws (Exodus 20:13–23:33) the people of Israel were given instruction regarding their relationships: Godward as well as toward others.

CHAPTER TWELVE

KADESH BARNEA

The months spent at the foot of Mount Sinai had been filled with activity. Using the gifts God had given them, the people had prepared the hangings, the coverings, the pillars, the furniture, and especially the Ark. When the Tabernacle had been erected and the Ark placed in the Holy of Holies, *Yahweh* showed His approval by coming and resting over the Holy of Holies. And Moses rejoiced because the Lord of Glory now resided in the midst of His people.[104]

His rejoicing, however, did not last for very long. Though the people had much for which to be truly grateful, they grumbled about what they did not have. They despised the manna, and complained because they did not have the variety of foods that had been available to them in Egypt (Numbers 11:1).[105] This angered the Lord, and He gave them something to complain about. He sent the fire of His judgment to burn up the tents of those on the outskirts of the camp. This destruction may have involved some of the peo-

---

104. Numerous books have been written on the Tabernacle. Two that are especially helpful to lay people are: J. Strong, *The Tabernacle of Israel* (Grand Rapids: Kregel, 1987), 166pp., and L. T. Talbot, *Christ in the Tabernacle* (Chicago: Moody, 1978), 285pp.

105. G. Bush, *Notes ... on the Book of Numbers* (Minneapolis: Klock & Klock, 1981), 146-53; R. K. Harrison, *Numbers*, Wycliffe Exegetical Commentary, 1990), 181-87.

ple as well. God's judgment on their ingratitude brought an immediate change of heart and, while the fire still burned, the people asked Moses to pray for them. He did so, and the fire died out.

Problems Along the Way (Numbers 11:1–12:16)

But the rabble (i.e., the "mixed multitude" who had tagged along with the Israelites when they left the land of slavery) influenced some of the Israelites, and together they voiced their dissatisfaction about their monotonous diet. Their whining showed how ungrateful they were for all of God's mercies, and they claimed that they had lost their appetite. They lusted for the buffet-style menus they said they had enjoyed in Egypt: fish and cucumbers and melons and leeks and onions and garlic.

The discontent of the rabble was most disturbing to Moses. He had been rejoicing over the way in which the Lord had been honored, and now, in the bitter complaint of the people, he felt that God was being dishonored. All that he had endured was now compounded by his disappointment, and this led him to voice a complaint of his own. He felt the task the Lord had given him was too demanding and too much for him to bear.

The Lord took this opportunity to remind Moses of the seventy men who had been chosen to share in the administration of the people. The time had come for them to assume their office. The Lord instructed Moses to assemble them outside the Tabernacle the next day, and there He would confirm them in their sacred office (Numbers 11:24-30).[106]

At the appointed time "*Yahweh* came down in the cloud and spoke with him, and He took the Spirit that was on Moses and put the Spirit on the seventy elders." This did not reduce Moses' power or authority, for the Holy Spirit possesses all of the attributes of the Godhead, including His omniscience, omnipresence and omnipotence. "When the Spirit rested on the seventy, they immediately prophesied, but they did not do so again." This phenomena accredited them in the new roll into which they had been inducted.

But what of the desire of the people for meat?

The Lord instructed Moses to say to the people, "Consecrate yourselves for tomorrow, and you shall eat meat; for you have wept in the hearing of *Yahweh*, saying, 'Who will give us meat to eat? For it was well with us in Egypt.' Therefore *Yahweh* will give you meat, and you shall eat. You shall eat, not one day, nor two days, nor five days, nor ten days, nor twenty days, but for a whole month, until it comes out of your nostrils and becomes loathsome to you, because you have despised *Yahweh* who is among you, and have wept before Him, saying, 'Why did we ever come up out of Egypt?'" (Num. 11:18-20)

Now the Lord caused a strong wind to blow that drove the quail in from the sea.[107] It brought them down all around the camp to about three feet above the ground, as far

---

106. Bush, *Numbers*, 162-65; Harrison, *Numbers*, 188-90.

as a day's walk in any direction. All that day and night and all the next day the people went out and gathered quail. No one gathered less than ten homers.[108]

Then they spread them out all around the camp to dry so that they would not rot.

The Lord, however, was angry with His people, for they had not asked Him to supply them with meat. Instead, they grumbled about the sameness of their diet, while minimizing all He had done for them. And so, while they were stuffing themselves with quail, the Lord sent a severe plague among the people, and many died.[109]

But this was not the end of Moses' trials. Aaron and Miriam took issue with him for having married a Cushite.

---

107. Quail usually migrate north in March-April and then fly south in August-September. They always fly with the wind. When flying over the sea they are subject to the shifting wind, and, when tired may fall into the sea and be drowned. The translation of Numbers 11:31 has caused confusion. From the time of Jerome (4th century) a theory was put forward (and it has since been accepted by most students of the Bible) that the quail flew about three feet above the ground and thus were easy for the Israelites to capture.

108. *Homer* (Heb. "heap," Leviticus 27:16; Numbers 11:32; Ezekiel 45:13. The homer contained ten ephahs (Ezekiel 45:11), nearly eight bushels.

109. A. Parmalee in *All the Birds of the Bible* (New Canaan, CT: Keats, 1959), 75-77 (see index for other references to quail).

"Has *Yahweh* spoken only through you?" they asked. "Hasn't He also spoken through us?"

The verb "spoke against" or "spoken through" is feminine singular, indicating that Miriam led in the criticism. The pretext used was Moses' marriage to a Cushite woman. The real reason for their overt hostility was jealousy. Seventy judges had been appointed by God, and they were anxious to avail themselves of the added authority.

The Lord severely rebuked them, and Miriam was punished with leprosy. Moses immediately requested that she be healed, but *Yahweh* insisted that she be sequestered for seven days outside the camp, and then be received back into the fold of Israel. His decision shows that the sin of criticism of God's servants is a serious matter. It can be forgiven, but it carries with it solemn consequences.

Problems at Kadesh Barnea (Numbers 13:1–14:45)

After receiving Miriam back into the fellowship of the nation of Israel the people moved on to Kadesh Barnea, a site in the Negev (or Southland) about 50 miles southwest of Beersheba and marked by four wells.[110] There the Lord told Moses to send twelve men—one from each tribe—into the land to determine what the land was like, the strength or

---

110. H. C. Trumbull, *Kadesh Barnea* (London: Hodder & Stoughton, 1884), 478pp., pages 272-73 leave little doubt that Trumbull and his associates found the original site from which the spies were sent into Canaan.

weakness of the people, their number, the fertility of the land, and the nature of their cities (Numbers 13:17-20).

A list is given of the leaders who were sent out. The names of most of them are unknown to us; but two, Caleb and Joshua, are worth remembering.

The spies set out, and we can imagine the mood of the people. Within a short time they would be entering the land God had promised to give them. And their discussion most likely ran along practical lines. The women may have been heard saying, "I want a spacious home, because I want to have lots of children;" and "I want my home near water." Among the men there was likely to be an emphasis on safety and rich fields in which their sheep and cattle could graze.

The spies took 40 days (almost six weeks) to spy out the land. The people in the Negev (Southland) were apprehensive with so many people camped in close proximity to their border, and so the spies may have avoided undue contact with them. They probably lived off the land and, as they journeyed north, kept a record of what they saw.

At the end of forty days they returned to Moses and the Israelites, and gave their report.

"We went into the land to which you sent us, and it does flow with milk and honey! Here is its fruit. But the people who live there are powerful, and the cities are fortified and very large. We even saw descendants of Anak there. The Amalekites live in the Negev; the Hittites, Jebusites and Amorites live in the hill country; and the Canaanites live near the sea and along the Jordan" (Numbers 13:27-30).

They also told of their visit to Hebron where the sons of Anak lived, and found out enough to identify them as descendants of the Nephilim.[111]

This report had the effect of instilling fear into the hearts of the people, and it was necessary for Caleb, one of the spies, to try to allay their fears. He said, "We should by all means go up and take possession of the land, for we shall surely overcome it."

But the men who had spied out the land contradicted Caleb, saying, "We are not able to go up against the people, for they are too strong for us." Then they added, "The land through which we have gone is a land that devours its inhabitants, and all the people whom we saw in it are men of great stature. There we saw the giants (the descendants of Anak who came from the giants); and we were like grasshoppers in our own sight, and so we were in their sight."

---

111. The Nephilim were men of huge stature (see Genesis 6:4). They are considered by many to be giant demigods, the unnatural offspring of the "daughters of men" (mortal women) in cohabitation with the "sons of God" (fallen angels). This utterly unnatural union violated God's created order, and necessitated the worldwide judgment of the Flood. (Note Genesis 6:4 where this unnatural cohabitation also took place after the Flood resulting in unusually large offspring.)

Caleb's appeal to the people to have faith in God's ability to do what seemed impossible, was contradicted by the most plausible unbelief.

The negative report of the ten spies impacted the Israelites, and they gave way to loud lamentation that continued on into the night. But this was not all. The Israelites turned on Moses and Aaron, and said, "If only we had died in Egypt! Or in this desert! Why did *Yahweh* bring us to this land only to let us fall by the sword? Our wives and children will be taken as plunder. Wouldn't it be better for us to go back to Egypt?" This led them to repudiate God's suzerainty over them, and they said to each other, "We should choose a leader and go back to Egypt" (cf. Numbers 14:2-4).

Before we go any further we need to analyze the dynamics of fear, and to do so we need to review what we have covered thus far.

Fear (in its many forms, from mild anxiety to outright panic) arises in our hearts when we attribute to a *person, place,* or *thing* two attributes that properly belong to God, *viz.,* almightiness (the power to take away our autonomy) and impendency (the power to do us harm).

- The Israelites claimed that as they explored the land they were intimidated by the inhabitants. "The *people* who live in the land are strong ... and there were there the Nephilim; and we became like grasshoppers in our own sight, and so were we in their sight" (Numbers 13:28, 33).

- They were also overawed by the cities (i.e., the *places*), and claimed that they were strong and too well fortified for individuals like themselves to capture.

- Finally, they added the *coup de grace* by saying that "the land devours its inhabitants." Whatever they meant by this was left unexplained.

The response of the people indicated the effect fear had on them. They said,

> "If only we had died in Egypt! Or in this desert! Why is *Yahweh* bringing us to this land only to let us fall by the sword? Our wives and children will be taken as plunder. Wouldn't it be better for us to go back to Egypt? We should choose a leader and go back to Egypt" (Numbers 14:2-4).

Significantly, the antidote to fear is to place ourselves unreservedly in God's hands and live within His sovereign will. The psalmist wrote of his experience in Psalm 46:1-3. When our trust is in the Lord we need have no fear, no matter what our outward circumstances![112]

---

112. See the author's *Unlocking the Scriptures* (Eugene, OR: Wipf and Stock, 2001), 175-88.

Note the encouragement given the people by Joshua and Caleb:

"The land, which we passed through to spy it out, is an exceeding good land. If *Yahweh* delights in us, then He will bring us into this land, and give it unto us; a land which flows with milk and honey. Only rebel not against *Yahweh*, neither fear the people of the land; for they are bread for us: their defense has been removed from over them, and *Yahweh* is with us: do not fear them" (Numbers 14:7-9).

For their faithful stand Joshua and Caleb were threatened with stoning, and they were only saved when *Yahweh* appeared in His glory in the Tabernacle. Of course, the history of martyrdom seldom has such dramatic intervention. On this occasion the Lord spoke to Moses and pronounced sentence on the unbelieving nation as well as on the unbelieving spies. The unbelieving nation would be kept out of Canaan for forty years (a year for each day the spies were in the land), and they would die in the desert (Numbers 14:33); and the spies who filled the hearts of the people with fear died of a plague that very day.

But what of Joshua and Caleb? They were men of faith and deserving of entrance into the land. They were kept out of the land because of the unbelief of the people, and for forty years shepherded their sheep in the desert. They, however, were promised an inheritance in the land with Hebron specifically being promised to Caleb.

Something to Think About

The late Dr. W. H. Griffith Thomas wrote the following based on Hebrews 3:7–4:12:

They came to the gates of Canaan,
   But they never entered in!
They came to the very threshold,
   But they perished in their sin.

On the morrow they would have entered,
   But God shut the gate;
They wept, they rashly ventured,
   But alas! It was too late.

And so we are ever coming
   To the place where the two ways part:
One leads to the land of promise,
   And one to a hardened heart.

CHAPTER THIRTEEN

WHEN TROUBLES MULTIPLY

As we near the end of our review of Moses' life and labors we would have expected that the trials he faced would have diminished. The very reverse was the case. His life illustrates for us that when a person lives a godly life he will most assuredly suffer from slander and opposition, and face threats from unexpected sources (cf. Christ's words in John 15:18–16:6).

Problems Arising From Within Israel (Numbers 16:1-50)

On this particular occasion Moses and Aaron were confronted by a coalition of prominent leaders from the tribes of Levi and Reuben. This formidable conspiracy was led by a man named Korah, and he was aided and abetted by Dathan, Abiram and On;[113] and behind them were 250 leaders of the people, "chosen in the assembly, men of renown."

The three reasons they gave for their revolt were as follows: (1) That Moses and Aaron had usurped authority beyond their due; (2) That the whole march had been a failure, for the comparative security and plenty of Egypt had been exchanged for the poverty of the wilderness, and the illursory promise of prosperity; and (3) That the priesthood

---

113. Inasmuch as On is not mentioned in 16:5ff. it is possible that he withdrew from the conspiracy.

was not a monopoly of the two brothers, but should be shared.

Korah was probably influenced by jealousy because the high honors and privileges of the priesthood had been exclusively appropriated by the family of Aaron (cf. Jude 1:11). Moses having supreme authority in civil affairs, it appeared to Korah and his followers that the power over the whole nation had been taken by him. The particular grievance that rankled Korah and his cronies was their exclusion from the office of the priesthood. They resented being confined to what they believed was the inferior service of the Tabernacle (cf. Numbers 4:2ff.), and totally overlooked the fact that God had appointed men in each family to these duties!

The next day the rebels presented themselves before the Tabernacle, along with Moses and Aaron. And the whole congregation gathered at the instigation of Korah. The Lord appeared and audibly commanded Moses and Aaron to separate themselves from the congregation, so that they might not share in its destruction for making common cause with the conspirators.

The two leaders prayed that the people might be spared, and that *Yahweh* would confine His wrath to the instigators of the rebellion. Instructed by Moses, the congregation withdrew. After that Moses depicted to what was about to happen as proof of his authority. The earth then opened up and swallowed Korah, Dathan, and Abiram, and their families. Then it closed over them. The other 250 rebels, who were probably in front of the Tabernacle, were then consumed by fire "from the Lord."[114]

One would have thought that such a demonstration of God's disapproval would have been sufficient to cause the people to acknowledge the respective positions of Moses and Aaron, and acknowledge their authority. But that was not what happened. Next, all the people gathered together and accused Moses and Aaron of killing the Lord's people! Their attention was suddenly diverted to the Tent of Meeting, where the cloud covered it and the glory of *Yahweh* appeared (Numbers 16:41-42). A plague then broke out among those who resented Moses' leadership, and 14,700 died.

The Momentary Lapse of Israel's Leader (Numbers 20:1-29)

The wandering of the Israelites brought them to the Wilderness of Zin. The punishment of the people for their unbelief at Kadesh Barnea was almost over. Miriam, Moses' and Aaron's sister, died at Kadesh from unspecified causes. In accordance with Hebrew tradition a period of mourning would have followed her burial. Though Miriam had not given her younger brother consistent support, she had played a prominent part in Israel's fortunes ever since they left Egypt. No eulogy was given her following her death.

The camp of Israel again grumbled and chided Moses for bringing them to a place where there was no water. The Lord had brought water from a rock before, and on this occasion Moses was confident that He would do the same again.

---

114. *Unger's New Bible Dictionary* (1966), 747.

Yahweh spoke to Moses from the Tabernacle, and said, "Take Aaron's rod, and you and your brother Aaron assemble the congregation and speak to the rock before their eyes, that its water may gush out." So Moses took Aaron's rod from before the Lord, and he and Aaron gathered the assembly before the rock. Then Moses said to them, "Listen now, you rebels; shall *we* bring forth water for you out of this rock?" and he struck the rock twice; and water gushed out.

The Lord, however, was not pleased with Moses (Numbers 20:12), and punished him by not allowing him to enter the land of Canaan. In hindsight, his sin was threefold: (1) Because he was no longer in control of his emotions, he disobeyed the specific command of God; (2) He sinned in his failure to give glory to God for the water that came from the rock; and (3) He sinned in exalting himself (and Aaron) by claiming power and authority that were not theirs. This comes out in his use of *"we"* in 20:10 ("must *we* bring you water out of this rock?").

Once the thirst of the people and their animals was quenched, they were satisfied for a time and were prepared to resume their march to the Plains of Moab.

Problems Arising From Without (Numbers 22:1-41)

It has been said by those who observe our human condition that "problems never come singly." Others, with equal validity, point out that "problems often come in threes." And so it seemed to Moses. He had brought God's people to the threshold of the Promised Land, and now they were faced with problems that were different from anything he had encountered before. They were not like the wars he and the people had fought, for they were precipitated by those who were not Israelites and directed against Israel's God.

Balak, king of Moab, was terrified by Israel's encampment near his domain, for he knew only too well what Israel had done to the Amorites (Numbers 21:21-35), and he feared that they might do the same to him and his people. He believed that if he could find a weakness in Israel's God, he could attack Israel and drive them from his land. He, therefore, sent for a prophet named Balaam. Now Balaam lived in *Abr Naharim*, the "land between the [Tigris and Euphrates] Rivers," in a town called Pethor (which has been identified by archaeologists as one of the leading centers of magic and the occult).

In order to win Balaam's services Balak began his message with flattery--"I know that he whom you bless is blessed, and he whom you curse is cursed." He then promised him enormous riches if he would come and curse the Israelites for him (Numbers 22:6). The envoy from Moab came to Balaam and passed on to him Balak's words. Balaam turned down Balak's offer, but invited Balak's representatives to spend the night with him, promising to relate to them anything which the Lord might say to him.

God came to Balaam during the night, and said, ""Who are these men with you?"

And Balaam answered and said, "Balak the son of Zippor, king of Moab, has sent them to me, saying, 'Look, a people has come out of Egypt, and they cover the face of the earth. Come now, curse them for me; perhaps I shall be able to overpower them and drive them out.'"

And God said to Balaam, "You shall *not* go with them; you shall *not* curse the people, for they are blessed."

So Balaam rose in the morning and said to the princes of Moab, "Go back to your land, for the Lord has refused to give me permission to go with you."

In this we have an example of God's specific and direct will.

Perhaps there was something tentative in Balaam's refusal to go with the ambassadors from Moab, for when they returned to Balak and told him what Balaam had said, Balak thought it was a ruse on Balaam's part to hold out for more money (Numbers 22:9-14). He, therefore, sent a second delegation, this time made up of more important ambassadors, who took with them greater wealth and made more lucrative promises.

Balaam should have declined Balak's overtures, but instead he invited the men to spend the night with him. His explanation was simple. It would give him the opportunity to consult the will of God once more. But Balaam was trying to cover that which he desired to do with a convenient act of piety. God knew of his hypocrisy and, in a vision of the night, said to him, "Inasmuch as the men have come to call you, rise and go with them; but only the word which I speak to you--that you shall do." So Balaam rose in the morning, saddled his donkey, and went with the delegation from Moab (Numbers 22:20-21).

In this we have an example of God's permissive will.

En route to the land of Moab the Angel of the Lord (i.e., the preincarnate Christ), knowing that Balaam had no real intention of saying only what *Yahweh* wanted him to say, met with him. The scene involved Balaam's donkey (Numbers 22:22-30), to which the Lord gave the special gift of speech. It must have been a humiliating experience for Balaam to be rebuked by his donkey, but it was only when the Lord opened Balaam's eyes and he saw the Angel of the Lord with His drawn sword, that he realized the seriousness of what he had planned to do (Numbers 22:31-35).

When Balak heard that Balaam was coming he went to the border of Moab, to the River Arnon, and personally welcomed the prophet. Balaam, of course, reiterated what he had already stated to the ambassadors, *viz.*, that he could speak only the words that God put in his mouth (Numbers 22:22-31).

That night Balak prepared a feast in honor of his guest, and he and the men with him dined in royal fashion. Then, the next morning he took Balaam to a hilltop from which vantage point the prophet could see the "utmost part" (i.e., the most remote part) of Israel's encampment. Balak's thought was evidently to show the weakest part of Israel's forces in the hope that Balaam would find it easy to curse them.

Balaam declined to curse God's people. The next morning Balak took Balaam to one of the religious sites of Baal; and there Balaam asked that seven altars be built, and seven bulls and seven rams be offered on these altars. Balak did so, and built similar altars for his sacrifices. In Balak's case he was invoking the power of his god, Molech, hoping to neutralize the power of Israel's God; in Balaam's case, he was trying to placate the true God with sacrifices in the hope that the Lord would relent and let him curse Israel (Numbers 23:3*b*-4).

When Balaam attempted to curse Israel, he blessed them instead (Numbers 23:7-10).

The same ritual was repeated on two more occasions, and Balaam's predictions were consistently for Israel's future blessing.[115]

In the end Balak became exasperated with Balaam's failure to do what he had been hired to do, and he expostulated, "Do not curse them at all nor bless them at all!" And Balaam went to his home on the banks of the River Euphrates, but not before he made one last attempt to obtain the silver and gold that Balak had promised him. He counseled Balak to have the Moabite women seduce the Israelite men

---

115. See Unger's *Commentary on the Old Testament*, 216-19; S. Cox, *Balaam, an Exposition and a Study* (London: Kegan Paul, Trench, 1884), 84-208; E. W. Hengstenberg, *Dissertations on the Genuineness of Daniel and the Integrity of Zechariah*, trans. by B. P. Pratten, and *Dissertation on the History and Prophecies of Balaam*, trans. by J. E. Ryland (Edinburgh: T. & T. Clark, 1847), 337-569.

into coming to a special feast held in their honor (Numbers 31:16).

Balaam knew that these festivities invariably degenerated into a sexual orgy, and was smart enough to know that eating meat sacrificed to heathen idols and engaging in promiscuous sex would bring down the judgment of God on Israel.

Some Things to Think About

Korah and His Company

The sin of covetousness, coupled with jealousy, probably influenced Korah and those with him to want the high honors and privileges of the priesthood that God had specifically assigned to the family of Aaron. They were rankled because–those among them who were Levites–had been assigned inferior service of the Tabernacle.

Scripture later affirms that the descendants of Korah became eminent in the Levitical service; it is clear that his sons were spared. They were probably living in separate tents or had separated themselves from the conspirators at the command of Moses.

This shows God's grace even in administering a most severe judgment, and His watchful care of those called into His service.

Moses' Angry Outburst

God's servants are not perfect, even though there are those who expect them to be free of all vices. As we have seen, Moses' disobedience was punished, even though he had been forgiven.

I tried, myself, to bring to pass
    That which I thought should be,
I felt the Lord would profit by
    A little help from me.
And so I worried and despaired
    And vainly labored on
Until my fairest plans had crashed,
    My choicest visions gone;
And then I knelt before my Lord,
    Chastened, humbled, still,
Ready to let Him work through me,
    Ready to do His will.
And there it was I found success.[116]

The Enigmatic Prophet From the Euphrates

Balaam was a "mugwump." A non-dictionary definition of a "mugwump" is someone who sits on the fence with

---

116. The poem is by Barbara E. Cornet. I have tried to find the copyright holder of this poem, but without success. If data can be procured, it will be provided in the next edition of this book.

his "mug" facing in one direction and his "wump" in the other.

A look at the some of the references to him in the New Testament reveal his weakness.

Balaam had some knowledge of the true God, and indeed sincerely desired to die the death of the righteous (Numbers 23:10), but he sinned against the light he had been given. The New Testament writers preserve information for us that, due to the brevity of the record was not included in the Old Testament. In 2 Peter 2:15 we read of the "*way* of Balaam;" in Jude 1:11 we learn of the "*error* of Balaam;" and in Revelation 2:14 we are warned about the "*doctrine* of Balaam."

The *way* of Balaam is the prostitution of one's gifts for base gain; the *error* of Balaam is the secret hope that the will of God can be circumvented under cover of an outward respect for His Word; and the *doctrine* of Balaam is the council Balaam gave Balak whereby the people of God could be ruined by introducing sexual promiscuity into their lifestyle (cf. Numbers 31:16).

Unhappily there are many leaders in our country who propagate these same errors.

CHAPTER FOURTEEN

THE SEDUCTION OF THE SONS OF ISRAEL

Whoever it was who first pointed out that trouble comes in threes, knew whereof he spoke. Israel had defeated the Canaanites at Arad and the Amorites in Heshbon and Bashan,[117] and were now happily ensconced on the fertile Plains of Moab. Across the River Jordan they could see the Promised Land, with the well-fortified city of Jericho nestling up against the mountains.

Israel's present situation was idyllic, and they had every reason to be happy. The countryside was carpeted with wild flowers that provided a kaleidoscope of color, and the land was watered by many small streams. Here and there grew stands of acacia trees where birds of the brightest plumage nested and raised their young. And farther south the scented oleanders added to what was already a picturesque panorama.

With such beauty all around them we are not surprised that the tribes of Reuben, Gad, and half of the tribe of Manasseh wished to stay on the eastern side of the River Jordan.

---

117. *Macmillan Bible Atlas* (1993), #52, p.48.

The Seduction (Numbers 25:1-3)

Balaam had returned to his home after Balak had rebuked him for not cursing the Israelites (Numbers 24:10-11, 25), and either while en route to Pethor or else when he was back in familiar surroundings, he came up with an idea that he felt sure would net him the wealth in silver and gold that Balak had at one time promised to give him.

Whatever the sequence of events, he hastily returned to Moab where he laid out his plan before Balak. His proposal was relatively simple. Balak should send nubile young women into the camp of the Israelites with the intent of inviting them to attend a feast in honor of the god who gave them prosperity. According to Numbers 25:18 these women used a variety of tricks to seduce the men of Israel. Their objective, of course, was to place the men in a compromising situation.[118]

The festivities began with drinking and dancing, and then degenerated into the kind of promiscuous orgy that broke down the walls of morality that had to this point surrounded the nation of Israel (cf. Joshua 13:22; Numbers 31:16).[119] Balaam knew that *Yahweh* was a forgiving God,

---

118. The festivities honored "Baal (i.e., lord) of Peor." For further information on the prevalence of Baal worship, see E. O. James, *The Ancient Gods* (London: Weidenfeld & Nicholson, 1960), 87-90; J. Gray, *The Legacy of Canaan*, Vetus Testamentum Supplement 5, rev. ed. (Leiden: Brill, 1965), 163-69; and J. C. L. Gibson, *Canaanite Myths and Legends*, 2d ed. (Edinburgh: Clark, 1978), 3-19.

but he also knew that He would not absolve those who were guilty of violating the covenant He had made with them (Exodus 34:7). Balaam's plan, therefore, was to induce Israel to break one or more of the commandments[120], whereupon a righteous God would be compelled to punish His people for their sins.

Judgment of the Transgressors (Numbers 25:4-9)

It was bad enough that the men of Israel "joined themselves to Baal"–an act which repudiated *Yahweh's* right to rule over them–but they were in danger of leading all God's people astray, for the sensuous acts of Baal-worship were more appealing than the limitations imposed by the ethical and moral principles of their true Suzerain (i.e., God). He, therefore, instructed Moses to "take all the leaders of the people and execute them in broad daylight before Me, so that My fierce anger may turn away from Israel."

Does this seem harsh?

The Israelites had willingly taken upon themselves obedience to the will of God (Exodus 19:5-6, 8). When they sinned and God announced their punishment, they had only themselves to blame.

---

119. Much like a Bacchanal.
120. When the Israelites allowed themselves to be seduced by the daughters of Moab, they broke the first and seventh commandments (Exodus 20:3 and 14).

The same decadence is still prevalent today. The walls of our society are crumbling, and the only hope for Western Civilization is to take a stand for the truth as it is found in God's Word, and repudiate the false teachings of those who "preach" a libertarian gospel.

In obedience to the word of the Lord, Moses said to the judges of Israel, "Each of you slay[121] his men who have joined themselves to Baal of Peor" (cf. Numbers 25:5). This was a powerful "object lesson," but one which the people of Israel would not soon forget.

The plague of Numbers 25:9 had already broken out among the people: and the more God-fearing among them had assembled at the door of the Tabernacle to intercede for mercy. While the people were weeping before the Lord a young man named Zimri, the son of Salu, a prince of a chief family in the tribe of Simeon (Numbers 25:14), brought a Midianite woman named Cozbi, daughter of Zur, head over a people of one of the chief families in Midian (Numbers 25:15), to meet his relatives.

These two persons had plainly entered into a matrimonial alliance, and its seriousness was aggravated because

---

121. The overtones of "being joined to Baal" reappear in the New Testament (see 2 Corinthians 6:14). The penalty for breaking their oath to *Yahweh* was death (see Bush, *Numbers*, 408, col. b). The offenders were probably stoned to death and then impaled or hanged on a tree until sundown (Deuteronomy 21:23). This public demonstration of God's judgment served as a deterrent to others not to commit similar sins.

one was a prince and the other a princess. Zimri's action was open, public and shameless, and after meeting with his relatives, he took Cozbi into the innermost part of his tent.

A priest named Phinehas, a descendant of Aaron, saw what was taking place, and, prompted by a sudden, holy zeal, took a spear and followed the couple into Zimri's tent. He found them in the inner chamber where the couple were already lying together. Phinehas disturbed their love-making by thrusting his spear through them both. With one stroke he left people from that time to the present with an illustration of how God views such sins.

And the plague that had already broken out ceased.

God's Praise of Phinehas' Zeal (Numbers 25:10-15)

Then *Yahweh* spoke to Moses, saying: "Phinehas the son of Eleazar, the son of Aaron the priest, has turned back My wrath from the children of Israel, because he was zealous with My zeal among them, so that I did not consume the children of Israel in My zeal. Therefore say, 'Behold, I give to him My covenant of peace; and it shall be to him and his descendants after him a covenant of an everlasting priesthood, because he was zealous for his God, and made atonement for the children of Israel.'"

For his selfless zeal the Lord gave Phinehas a "covenant of peace," implying abundant prosperity and his life crowned with a fulness of blessing, both temporal and spiritual. Dr. George Bush paraphrases the Lord's intent: "Let him know that by way of reward for so noble and pure an example of religious zeal, a zeal not prompted by private passion, by hasty, uncharitable, or ungovernable resentment, but by a solid and earnest regard to the honor of divine majesty, the love of truth, and the highest welfare of his brethren, his family shall, in the direct line from him, be honored with the privilege of a long succession in the high priesthood ..."[122]

The War Against the Midianites (Numbers 25:16-18; 31:1-54)

God's people were punished for their unfaithfulness, and 42,000 new graves were dug on the Plains of Moab. But that did not mean that His honor was to be unavenged. He spoke to Moses, and said, "Be hostile to the Midianites and strike them; for they have been hostile to you with their tricks, with which they have deceived you in the affair of Peor and in the affair of Cozbi, the daughter of the leader of Midian, their sister who was slain on the day of the plague because of Peor."

It was to avenge this plot that the last war of Moses was undertaken. God's specific command still protected Moab, but Midian, which had been Moab's willing accomplice, received the chastisement that both deserved.

One thousand warriors were selected from every tribe throughout the tribes of Israel, and to this small representative army was committed the task of defeating the myriads of Midian. Phinehas was appointed to accompany the expe-

---

122. G. Bush, *Numbers*, 412, col. a.

dition, and he took with him the Ark of the Covenant and vessels of the Sanctuary, and the sacred trumpets.

The Midianite army was commanded by five chiefs, each of whom had the title of "king" (but were probably heads of tribes like Oreb and Zeeb, Zebah and Zalmunna, cf., Judges 8:3-5). And in all likelihood Moab sent a contingent under Balaam. We deduce this, because he was present and took part in the battle which resulted in the demise of Midian's chiefs and resulted in his death as well (Joshua 13:22). Far from "dying the death of the righteous," Balaam came to an ignominious end.

An enormous quantity of spoil was taken, besides a great quantity of golden armlets and bracelets, signet rings, earrings and necklaces (Numbers 31:32-35). All male Midianites and all women who were not virgins were to be killed, for they might endanger the inheritance of Israel's sons. All the spoils had to be purified–that which could not withstand fire had to be subjected to water mixed with the ashes of a red heifer, and that which could withstand fire, by fire and water.

The spoils were to be divided equally between those who fought and those who remained in the camp. The soldiers were to dedicate one out of every 500 captured persons and animals to the Lord, and from the gold taken from the Midianites they offered to the Lord a vast sum estimated at 6,700 ounces.[123] This munificent gift showed their gratitude to the Lord for giving them the victory.

---

123. See the *Ryrie Study Bible*, 262-63.

Something to Think About

Victory in the Christian life (cf. chs. 22–24) may be followed by defeat. It is necessary for us, therefore, to be aware of Satan's devices (2 Corinthians 2:11), and live under the authority of God's Word.

In Phinehas we see the power of a godly example. He stood boldly for the truth and took courageous action. In what way was he motivated by well defined spiritual principles? Can you think of other biblical examples?

Balaam, who cared more for riches than living up to the light God gave him, never lived to enjoy the riches that Balak gave him. Though he fondly desired to die the death of the righteous (cf. Numbers 23:10), he died with the enemies of the Lord. In what ways does his death reveal God's sovereignty on the one hand, and the awfulness of His just retribution on the other?

Lastly, let us note the response of grateful hearts illustrated for us in the gift of 6,700 ounces of gold that Israel gave to the Lord. In what ways may we show our gratitude to the Lord for all His goodness to us (cf. Psalm 50:23)?

CHAPTER FIFTEEN

"CLIMBING ON TRACK"

I met Fred Mitchell soon after becoming a Christian. He was busy raising support for the China Inland Mission (later renamed the Oriental Mission Fellowship). It was a memorable encounter. Within a few weeks he took off for the Far East. Less than a year later news flashed around the world that the airplane Fred Mitchell was on had been lost. It had taken off from Singapore en route to New Delhi when all communication with the aircraft was suddenly cut short. The last message sent out was "Climbing on Track."

The wreckage of the downed aircraft was found twenty-two miles northwest of Calcutta. There were no survivors.

Phyllis Thompson, who wrote a biography about Fred Mitchell--the pharmacist, lay preacher, mission director, conference speaker, and family man--took the last words from the cockpit of the fated airplane *"Climbing on Track"* as the best way to sum up his brief, yet moving story. And, for our purpose, the title of her book also captures the essence of the life and labors of Moses, the Servant of the Lord.

God's Message (Numbers 20:2-13; 27:12-14)

Because Moses struck the rock with Aaron's rod instead of speaking to it, he had disobeyed the explicit command of the Lord. Though the Lord gave His people their much needed water, He told Moses that for this act of unrighteous anger he would not be permitted to cross the River Jordan into the land of Canaan.

But this was not all. The Lord also told him that Israel was to fight against the Midianites, and after that he would die and be gathered to his people. His astonishing career was coming to an end.

Dr. E. M. Blaiklock wrote somewhat pessimistically that "death in those days held none of the clear hope" which we read about in the New Testament. Yet it must be borne in mind that Moses, who had known God well, had no doubts about life beyond the grave.[124] And even before his time the patriarchs had held fast to faith in the Lord. That is why the writer of Hebrews could state emphatically,

> These all died in faith, not having received the promises, but having seen them afar off were assured of them, embraced them and confessed that they were strangers and pilgrims on the earth. For those who say such things declare plainly that they seek a homeland.... a heavenly country. Therefore God is not ashamed to be called their God, for He has prepared a city for them (Hebrews 11:13-16).

Moses could not have sustained the burden of leading all the people were it not for his abiding faith in the God of his fathers. But there is more. A careful reading of Psalm 90 impresses upon our minds Moses' concern for his people

---

124. Blailock, *Bible Characters*, 86.

and for a godly leader to succeed him. The choice, as we know, fell to Joshua (Numbers 27:15-23), and after Moses had inducted him into his new office in the presence of the people, he was ready to pass from this life into the next.

According to the Jewish historian, Josephus,[125] Moses withdrew from the camp without fanfare, but the people who saw him lined the path he took shedding copious tears with the women beating their breasts to show their grief. The children also gave way to uncontrolled weeping as they saw Moses, his physical abilities unabated, stride resolutely to the base of the 2,500-foot mountain chain and there he began his final ascent.

At a certain point he turned and made a sign to the grief-stricken people below indicating that they should advance no further. He then continued on his upward climb with the elders, the high priest, and Joshua as his only attendants. At the top of the mountain he dismissed the elders, and was proceeding to embrace Eleazar and Joshua when a cloud covered him, and he vanished from their sight.

The Death of Moses (Deuteronomy 34:1-12)

Two things only remained for Moses to do. First, as a mark of God's grace, he was to take a long, satisfying look at the Promised Land. With clear and unclouded sight (see Deuteronomy 34:7) he feasted his eyes on the tents of Israel far below him, and then looked with rapt attention at the "goodly land" to which he had brought his people, which he

---

125. Josephus, *Antiquities of the Jews*, IV: 8: 48.

knew would be their inheritance. He then looked to the north and the west, the south and the east, and took in the beauties of what God had promised to give to His people (cf. Deuteronomy 3:25, 27).

Across the River Jordan he could see the stately palm trees that marked the spring outside the city of Jericho, the key to the Land of Promise. And beyond Jericho there was spread the whole range of mountains: All of Gilead with Mts. Hermon and Lebanon in the east and north; the hills of Galilee overhanging the pear-shaped Lake of Gennesareth; the wide opening that gave access to the Valley of the Esdraelon; the rounded summits of Ebal and Gerizim; and in the foreground Mt. Zion, and a little farther south Bethlehem sitting on top of a narrow limestone ridge. And, as he gazed down, he saw seemingly beneath his feet the valley through which flowed the River Jordan.[126]

Jewish legends elaborate upon the death of Moses, but the actual manner of his passing remains a mystery. No eye saw it, and no one knew the exact moment of it. In silence and solitude, alone with God at the top of Mt. Nebo, the great lawgiver and leader of his people, passed away.

Scripture affirms that when Moses died the devil wanted to take his body, but Michael the archangel opposed him and called upon the Lord to rebuke him (Jude 1:9). Joshua, writing under inspiration of the Holy Spirit, records

---

126. Visitors to the Holy Land have amplified what Moses probably saw, see Stanley's *Jewish Church* (1875), 167-68.

that it was the Lord who buried Moses, and that no mortal man knows the place of His burial (Deuteronomy 34:5-6).

The children of Israel wept for Moses for thirty days, but there were no funeral rites and no monument erected to his memory.

And so the "servant of the Lord" died (Exodus 14:31; Numbers 7:7; Deuteronomy 34:5; Joshua 1:1). The special attributes that might have been engraved on a tombstone would have testified to his unswerving faithfulness--the kind of unshaken fidelity that characterized his entire life. And so the writer of Hebrews could unashamedly write, "he was faithful in all God's house" (Hebrews 3:5).

As we look back on his leadership of the people through the "great and terrible wilderness," we see him time and again either encouraging the people (as at the Red Sea, Exodus 14:13, 14; Deuteronomy 1:30), or explaining what the Lord was doing (cf. Exodus 16:6, or 15), or reproving them for their disobedience (cf. Exodus 17:2; Numbers 14:41; Deuteronomy 4:31). Only once did the strain of command cause him to give way to anger (Numbers 20:10-13), and even then we can empathize with him for he had borne their incalcitrance for forty years.

The second characteristic that impresses itself upon us is his meekness. As we pointed out earlier, a good definition of "meekness" is "strength under control." Moses was not a placid, tame Casper Milktoast, but a man who could be quickly provoked by the wrongful actions of others. Illustrations of this may be seen in his hasty killing of the Egyptian (Exodus 2:12), vigorous defense of the daughters of Jethro (Exodus 2:17-19), and hasty breaking of the tablets containing the Law of the Lord (Exodus 32:19).

But these early acts must be placed alongside his defense of the honor of the Lord; quick, prayerful response when the Lord wanted to wipe Israel off the face of the earth, gracious treatment of Miriam when she openly opposed him, and mild rebuke of Aaron when Aaron failed in the trust that had been given him. And, of course, other examples could be multiplied ad infinitum.

Moses' meekness reveals his bridled strength, and illustrates for us the strengths and weaknesses of the servants of the Lord.

Before we close this general discussion of the life and labors of Moses, I need to share something that has become increasingly important. In the early years of my ministry I often became embroiled in controversial discussions with "thin-ice conservatives" or quasi-evangelicals on the subject of the inspiration and inerrancy of the Scriptures. One of their strategies was to challenge the authorship of certain points of Scripture (e.g., ascribing the book of Deuteronomy to Moses, and then asking how Moses could write of his death when he was already dead)?

The answer is quite simple. The Holy Spirit is the Author of Scripture, and He can inspire whom He will to write whatever He wishes. Examples of this are to be found in 2 Timothy 3:16; and 2 Peter 1:21. An appropriate lay definition would involve certain elements: God the Holy Spirit is the Author; He superintends the human authors whom He has chosen to write what He desires, and the human writers were conscious of writing Scripture (cf. 1 Corinthians 2:13; 1 Peter 1:11-12).

The doctrine of inspiration extends to the original documents.

Further validation comes from the use of Old Testament quotations in the New Testament.

How important has the inspiration and inerrancy of Scripture become? About a decade ago several thousand pastors were asked in a poll about their churches and their ministry. When the results were analyzed it was found that 49% did not believe the Bible was the Word of God. The question then must be asked, What kind of teaching did these pastors share with their congregations Sunday-by-Sunday?

The words of Dr. Charles C. Ryrie need to be internalized and the teaching of Scripture put into practice in one's daily life. Dr. Ryrie wrote: "The Bible is the greatest of all books; to study it is the noblest of all pursuits; to understand it is the highest of all goals."[127]

Something to Think About

Moses had brought the Israelites to Kadesh Barnea. The land God had promised to them lay before them. Why

---

127. "To the Reader," *Ryrie Study Bible*, new edition.

did they turn away?   What part did fear play in their decision?

In the land of Moab God's people succumbed to idolatry. They were also seduced by the Moabite women. How might the lessons of the past have helped them and prevented many of them from dying?

Was Moses an equitable lawgiver (see Numbers 36:1-13)?

How did Moses acquire the characteristics of humility? What does the Bible teach us about humility?

How would you define meekness? Was the Lord Jesus meek?

What do these traits of humility and meekness have to do with the gifts of the Holy Spirit?